Communication at Work

THE SUNDAY TIMES

Communication at Work

Judith Taylor

△ KOGAN PAGE | *CREATING SUCCESS*

other titles in the Kogan Page creating success series

With grateful thanks to family, friends and colleagues who have helped with the preparation of this book, both directly through interviews and indirectly through ideas and advice.

First published in 2001

Apart from any fair dealing for the purposes of research or private study, or criticism or review, as permitted under the Copyright, Designs and Patents Act 1988, this publication may only be reproduced, stored or transmitted, in any form or by any means, with the prior permission in writing of the publishers, or in the case of reprographic reproduction in accordance with the terms and licences issued by the CLA. Enquiries concerning reproduction outside these terms should be sent to the publishers at the undermentioned address:

Kogan Page Limited
120 Pentonville Road
London N1 9JN
UK

© Judith Taylor, 2001

The right of Judith Taylor to be identified as the author of this work has been asserted by her in accordance with the Copyright, Designs and Patents Act 1988.

The views expressed in this book are those of the author, and are not necessarily the same as those of Times Newspapers Ltd.

British Library Cataloguing in Publication Data

A CIP record for this book is available from the British Library.

ISBN 0 7494 3474 0

Typeset by Jean Cussons Typesetting, Diss, Norfolk
Printed and bound in Great Britain by Clays Ltd, St Ives plc

contents

introduction

This book, part of the Creating Success series, is aimed at new and inexperienced managers. Modern electronic communications have transformed office life, and there is a danger that interpersonal skills are being neglected. It is therefore very important that people entering management today ensure that they are confident in their ability to communicate effectively in a variety of ways, and that the benefits and dangers of office technology are recognised.

The book takes the view that we can all communicate effectively, as long as we recognise that important skills are involved, which should be developed and practised. It looks at some of the changes affecting the modern office, and then takes managers through different forms of communication, including the telephone, writing, face-to-face communication and e-mail. The importance of training to enhance professionalism is also covered.

changes in office work

There is much talk of the paperless office but in practice most organisations work with a variety of paper-based and electronic media. However, the effects of the electronic revolution have been profound and have affected all aspects of office life. Information can be accessed easily, transmitted to many people simultaneously and responded to almost immediately, and expectations build up that enquiries and demands will all be treated as matters of urgency. Information is available to all, not just to the experts. A recent survey by the Institute of Management found that 85 per cent of managers think that they now have much more information to deal with than they used to have.

In most offices there is constant pressure to reduce costs and maximise profits or, in the public sector, give greater value for money for the services provided. This is leading to a short-term focus on immediate results, a decrease in the number of permanent employees and an increasing number of people employed on short-term contracts. People no longer expect to stay in the same job for life, and individuals are expected to manage their own careers. Opportunities for organisations to 'grow' promising individuals over a period of time are more limited, and the priority for managers is to ensure that their subordinates are equipped to do their current job as well as possible; longer-term career development is the responsibility of the individual.

Restructuring is also common – the same report by the Institute of Management found that 67 per cent of respondents had experienced some form of organisational change in the past year. The jobs themselves have become more flexible, often project-based, with attendant difficulties for managers. E-mail, electronic diaries, mobile telephones and the Internet have made it possible for multi-site and home working. Greater individual autonomy over work and easy access to information by non-specialists, in the context of wider changes in society at large, have resulted in a reduction of hierarchies and more questioning of authority. The jobs of managers have become more fragmented, and in many ways more complex; the old ways of managing by diktat are no longer appropriate, and managers have to learn new ways of working with an autonomous, flexible, project-based workforce. Interestingly, the Institute of Management survey found that 64 per cent of respondents thought the amount of time spent on organisational politics had greatly increased.

People work independently and there is less secretarial support. Open-plan offices and hot-desking are common (hot-desking is when desks or work stations are shared among part-time or peripatetic workers). This can cause difficulties for organisations wishing to build loyalty among their staff and for managers of teams who may have infrequent face-to-face contact with one another unless arrangements are made to bring people together from time to time.

In this situation managers need to be flexible in their approach, and learn to manage through empowerment rather than control. Training is more important than ever, for both managers and individuals. In the Institute of Management survey, 71 per cent of respondents thought they needed a broader range of skills than they used to, especially 'better developed interpersonal skills'. New ways of working can only be effective if people have the skills and knowledge necessary to do the job and if these are regularly updated in a fast-changing environment.

With all the emphasis on information technology, there is a danger that we will produce a workforce of IT haves and have-nots; already there is dissatisfaction among those who are not IT-literate and do not have access to computers. An organisation that cares for its workers will seek to provide access to IT and training for all its staff, even those who do not currently need it for their work.

professionalism and communication at work

professionalism

We have seen how many of the changes described in the Introduction have led to a greater individual autonomy over work. Most people take a pride in their work, and like to do things well. However, they don't always appreciate the effects of what they say and do on other people, and may need to be alerted to this. It is often the more junior staff who have most frequent contact with members of the public, and bear a big responsibility for conveying a positive, helpful, efficient image of the organisation. Standards and expectations and levels of authority, responsibility and control should be clarified and agreed with each member of staff, and training provided to develop skills and confidence.

We all need to think about who we are communicating with, and why. A flexible style, which can be adapted according to circumstances, is important, but it should always be polite, tactful and clearly expressed. And we should never forget that we represent our organisation. The impression that an individual makes contributes to the overall image of the organisation, and if that is a positive one it will bring long-term benefits to everyone.

Working independently doesn't mean working in isolation. It calls for greater efforts to communicate with colleagues, keeping them informed, making them feel valued, emphasising the role that each member plays in the achievement of goals and the overall success of the team. It is important to make an effort to meet with people, to pick up the telephone from time to time and to devise activities that will boost morale, encourage team spirit and avoid the dangers of isolation.

communication

People communicate at work for a variety of reasons by means of the spoken word, the written word, non-verbal communication, numbers, drawings and graphics, using a wide range of media including the telephone, face-to-face meetings, video-conferencing, e-mail, letters and memos. Skilled communicators consider which is the most appropriate medium for the particular message they wish to convey.

It's always easier to criticise other people's communication skills rather than our own. Most of us probably think we are good communicators – it's other people who are the problem! However, managers in particular need to evaluate critically their own skills and work on improving them.

Good communication requires patience, skill and commitment. The need is for:

- accuracy in order to send clear, precise messages;
- sensitivity to the feelings and opinions of the person to whom the message is being sent;
- skill in transmission (ie the ability to say what you want in the most appropriate way).

We communicate in order to understand and be understood; this is therefore a two-way process. It requires a message to be sent to a recipient, and that message to be received and understood. In order to discover if it has been received and, if so, whether it has been properly understood, you also need feedback. In other words, the other person might say 'Yes', 'I see', 'I understand' or, conversely, 'I don't understand', in which case you have to try to convey your message more clearly. One-way message giving and two-way communication are illustrated in Figure 1.1.

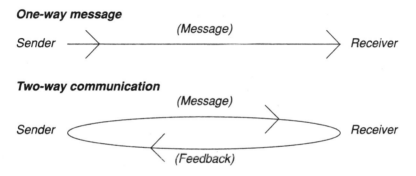

Figure 1.1 *One-way message and two-way communication*

Feedback also allows the receiver of the message to comment on it in some way, and a dialogue may ensue. Most of the time we give and receive feedback naturally, without thinking about it, using a range of verbal and non-verbal signs and signals to show that we are participating in the communication process. However, it is worth teasing out some of the key skills involved so that we can begin to understand how to put things right when they go wrong. Skills that are appropriate in all oral communication are awareness and the appropriate use of body language, listening, questioning, responding, summarising and assertiveness.

⟨ body language

Feedback is easier in face-to-face communication than it is on the telephone, or in writing. In face-to-face conversation we learn a great deal above and beyond the words being used, from facial expression, the way people use their hands, shrug their shoulders, or shuffle their feet. This is known as body language, or non-verbal communication, and it includes all those things that add meaning to what we say in addition to the words used. It is particularly significant in conveying feelings and attitudes.

Research conducted by Professor A Mehrabian (1971) in the United States suggests that three dimensions of human feelings and attitudes are often communicated more effectively through non-verbal cues: like–dislike; potency or status (power); and responsiveness. The research also indicates that the total impact of a message is: 7 per cent – words only; 38 per cent – vocal (eg tone of voice); and 55 per cent – non-verbal (especially facial expressions). The research has been criticised for simplifying some complex processes, but the general point holds, that body language is a very important part of the communication process.

For much of the time, our gestures, facial expressions and tone of voice add to or enhance what we are saying. We smile to convey pleasure, frown when unhappy, open our arms to indicate size, shout when angry. Difficulties arise, however, when there is a lack of congruence between what we say and how we say it. So, for example, if you ask people whether they have understood an instruction you have given, and they mutter 'yes' but don't meet your eyes, shuffle their feet and look unhappy, the chances are that they haven't understood but don't like to say so.

Your awareness and understanding of body language will improve interpersonal communications at two levels. On the one hand, you must make sure that your body language is congruent with the content of what you are saying. It's no good having a serious talk with your staff about timekeeping if you use a hesitant tone of voice and finish with a smile and a little laugh. Equally, as shown in the example above, you need to be alert to the non-verbal cues that other people exhibit in order to understand what they are really wanting to say.

listening

You may wonder why listening warrants a separate section to itself. Surely everyone can listen. The answer is that everyone can hear, unless they have a physical disability, but few people listen well, and most of us can develop and improve our skills. If people think you are not listening to them – ignoring them – they are likely to feel resentful. They may become reticent, or angry, or demotivated. On the other hand, if your team are confident that you are listening carefully and empathetically they will accept that you may not be able to solve all their problems.

First of all, let's look at some of the obstacles to good listening. There may be external distractions, like noise, or visual distractions such as someone moving about. You may be listening to a person who speaks very quietly, or indistinctly, or with a strong accent. Or there may be distractions that are personal to you. Some will be primarily physical; perhaps you are feeling hungry, or tired, or worried about some overdue accounts. Perhaps there are urgent matters that you must attend to as soon as the speaker has had his or her say. It's all too easy to let a chance word trigger off a train of thought that has nothing to do with the subject under discussion. They are rare people who can put their hand on their heart and say they have never done this; have never come to with a start and realised that they have missed some important information through sheer inattention.

Perhaps you are so eager to share your ideas that you interrupt without hearing the other person out. There are positive aspects to this – it's good to have ideas – but interrupting other people suggests a lack of respect for them and their views, and you may miss something important. Laziness may cause you to listen selectively, or not at all. You may lose track by starting to debate the ideas in your own head, or concentrate too much on the detail rather than the overall message.

The most difficult distractions to deal with are psychological ones. There is security in holding on to what you already know, and a certain amount of anxiety may be expected when you receive new information. You may stop listening because you think you've heard it all before, because you have already anticipated what the speaker is going to say, or because you disagree with what the speaker is saying. A good discipline is to make yourself listen to someone whose views you disagree with. Next time a politician from a party that you don't support appears on television, instead of switching channels practise listening. To see how successful you have been, summarise it to a friend, or in writing. Then, think about what you did in order to help yourself to listen and make sure that you practise these skills in future.

So what do we do about distractions? Well, don't pretend they aren't there. Acknowledge the external and the physical distractions, and try to set them aside. Remind yourself that it is important for you to listen, and that this will require energy and commitment. Try to be open-minded about controversial subjects.

Motivation is the key to good listening. Motivation means wanting to listen, being prepared to set aside distractions, and concentrating all your attention on the speaker. Listen for ideas, take notes and practise active listening. There may, of course, be occasions when the distractions are such that you really cannot listen, in which case try to negotiate a postponement of the discussion to a more convenient time.

Active listening is a way of engaging with the other person, being receptive to what he or she is saying and showing that you are listening. This not only increases your concentration but encourages the other person to continue talking. You practise active listening by checking your understanding from time to time ('Am I right in thinking that...?'), summarising what is agreed ('So we're agreed that we'll meet again next Thursday, and you'll notify your colleagues...?') and clarifying points of disagreement. You can also use body language (see above). Guidelines for listening skills are set out in Table 1.1.

Table 1.1 *Guidelines for listening skills*
(amended from an unknown source)

	The Active Listener	The Passive Listener
Body Language	Adopts positive posture; avoids distracting mannerisms; maintains reasonable eye contact; uses encouraging gestures and facial expression as appropriate; maintains comfortable distance.	Looks bored or judgemental; doodles or fiddles distractingly; avoids eye contact; shows little response to what is being said.
Attention	Keeps attention focused on speaker: 'When that happened, what did you do?'	Keeps focus of comments on self: 'When something like that happens to me, I...'
Accepting	Accepts speaker's ideas and feelings: 'That's an interesting idea. Can you say more about it?'	Fails to accept speaker's ideas and feelings: 'I think it would be better to...'
Empathy	Empathises: 'So when that happened, you felt that.'	Fails to empathise: 'I don't see why you felt annoyed.'
Questions	Uses open questions; probes in a helpful way: 'Could you tell me more about...?'	Uses closed questions; fails to probe.
Clarifies	Asks for clarification; checks understanding by paraphrasing, etc.	Assumes things; fails to clarify; fails to check understanding.
Summarises	Summarises progress from time to time; widens range of ideas by summarising a number of alternatives from which the speaker can choose.	Fails to summarise; narrows range of ideas by suggesting a 'correct' course of action.

A really skilled listener listens on several different levels – for the facts, the thoughts, the feelings and the intention. For example, someone stops you in the corridor to tell you a long story about the difficulty he had getting into work that morning. This could be a simple description – the person simply wanted to have a chat. On the other hand, he may want to tell you why he is late in, that he is feeling cross and frustrated, and his intention is to let you know that he is unable to settle down to work immediately. At a different level it could be a precursor to telling you that he is really fed up with travelling and is about to look for another job closer to home.

asking questions

People are sometimes reluctant to ask questions. This may be because asking for information seems like an admission of ignorance, because they don't like or are otherwise uncomfortable with the person they must ask, or because they are diffident about making a direct approach. Naturally, you should try to avoid taking up the time of busy people if you can find out the answer for yourself. However, it is far better to ask and get it right than guess and risk getting it wrong.

As a manager, you are likely to spend a substantial amount of time asking questions of one kind or another. You may require information from a range of different people – subordinates, senior managers, colleagues, clients, competitors. You will need to be able to phrase your questions to suit the circumstances.

Anyone who has been involved in selection interviews, for example, will know that it is not easy to get the information you need out of each candidate in a short space of time. Asking the right question in the right way at the right time is an important skill, although it is not always recognised as such.

The main types of question are set out in Table 1.2, with an indication of their usefulness.

Table 1.2   *The main types of question and their usefulness*
(amended from an unknown source)

Question	Useful	Not useful
Open: 'Tell me about...?' Encourage the person to talk.	Most openings; to explore and gather information.	With talkative person; where discipline is required.
Probing: 'Exactly what happened next?' Vital for detail.	Checking information.	Exploring emotionally charged areas.
Closed: 'What time did you start?' Narrow; establish specific points of fact.	Probing single facts.	Gaining information in areas not normally explored by interviewer.
Reflective: 'You feel upset about the move...' Very powerful; repeat back verbatim the emotional content of a statement.	Problem solving; emotionally charged situations; counselling.	Checking information and fact.
Leading: 'I expect you wish you'd allowed more time?' Invariably leads to the answer you expect.	Gaining acceptance of your view.	Gaining any information about person.
Hypothetical: 'What would you do if...?' Posing a hypothetical situation in the future.	Getting someone to think about new ideas.	With someone who needs time to give a reasoned reply.
Multiple: String of questions or statements.	Never.	Always.

It is worth spending some time thinking about the questions you ask in order to elicit information from people. You can't script a complete conversation, but you can plan your opening question, together with a few further key questions to include as appropriate. In many cases a useful pattern is to start with an open question to get the conversation going and to learn about the situation in broad terms, and then narrow the topic down with probing and closed questions in order to check the facts. For example, you might say, 'Tell me about the new process', followed by 'What part do you play in this?' then 'Were you trained to use the machine?' Don't forget that how you ask is as important as what you ask. A simple question such as 'Why did you do that?' can be asked in a variety of ways to indicate simple curiosity, anger, sarcasm, etc, depending on which words you emphasise and your tone of voice.

assertiveness

Assertiveness is an important skill. Before reading any further, try to answer the questions in the following exercise.

exercise – how assertive are you?

(Score on a scale of 1–3: 3 = often; 2 = sometimes; 1 = never)

1. In meetings I am able to speak up with confidence.
2. I can ask for help with something I am unsure about without feeling embarrassed.
3. I can express disagreement without getting defensive or angry.
4. With my manager, I can be open and honest about any difficulties I am facing, such as feeling put down or taken for granted.
5. With subordinates, I can give criticism in a constructive way.
6. I am able to give praise to colleagues, where due.
7. I can say no to a request without feeling guilty.
8. I can accept others saying no to a request from me.
9. If someone asks my opinion about something I feel

quite comfortable to give it even if I think my
opinion will not be a popular one.

10. When making a complaint about a service I can
state my case well without aggression.

11. When I see a problem I can draw attention to
it early without waiting until it becomes a crisis.

12. When I have bad news to give, I can do so calmly
and empathetically without excessive worry.

13. If I want something I can ask for it in a direct,
straightforward way.

14. When someone misunderstands me I can point it
out without making the other person look foolish.

15. When I disagree with the majority view I can state
my case without apologising or being
confrontational.

16. I take criticism well.

17. I can challenge patronising or manipulative
behaviour without getting angry.

18. I can express emotion without feeling embarrassed
or defensive, and without making others feel
guilty.

Total

How to score:
40–54 You are confident and assertive in your approach to situations.
30–39 Although you can be assertive you could develop your skills further.
18–29 You need to do some work in order to be more consistent in your assertive behaviour.

Assertiveness is a term that is used to describe a way of dealing with people that is open and honest without being either passive or aggressive. It is a communication skill that enables you to state your needs, feelings and opinions clearly and openly and negotiate with others to reach a mutually satisfactory outcome. By communicating assertively you are less likely to misunderstand or be misunderstood. Assertive behaviour allows you to:

- express disagreement without creating unnecessary conflict;
- make requests and state views in a confident manner;
- co-operate with others in solving problems so that everybody is reasonably satisfied with the outcome;
- cope with criticism;
- deal with awkward people and awkward situations more effectively.

The objective is not to get your own way at all costs, but to try to reach a mutually satisfactory outcome.

Practising assertiveness will help you to deal with difficult situations both at home and at work. People sometimes confuse assertiveness with aggression, or with getting your own way regardless, so let's look at some definitions. *Assertiveness* is a form of behaviour and a communication tool that involves standing up for your own rights without violating those of other people, and expressing yourself in direct, honest and appropriate ways. It is based on the belief that:

You have needs to be met	So do others
You have rights	So do others
You have something to contribute	So do others

Non-assertiveness, on the other hand, means that you put other people before yourself at all times, and fail to stand up for your rights or express your needs.

Aggression means that you always put yourself first, disregarding others and ignoring the fact that they may have needs, rights and contributions to make.

A right is something to which you are entitled. There are three kinds: legal rights, enshrined in the law of the land; job rights, concerning your contract of employment, working conditions, entitlement to study leave, etc; and general rights, which have been developed from the Universal Declaration of Human Rights agreed by the United Nations in 1948.

There is no definitive list, but assertive rights generally include:

- the right to be treated with respect;
- the right to have and express your own feelings and opinions;
- the right to be listened to and taken seriously;
- the right to state your own needs and set your own priorities;
- the right to say 'no' without feeling guilty;
- the right to ask for what you want;
- the right to say 'I don't understand';
- the right to make mistakes and take responsibility for them;
- the right to choose not to assert yourself.

Your own personal beliefs will affect your ability to be assertive, and the rights you feel able to accept or give to others. Beliefs are things we hold to be true about other people, and about ourselves. They are difficult to change. Beliefs we hold about ourselves include the sort of person we think we are ('I'm very shy', 'I'm a bad-tempered person'), what we are prevented from doing ('I can't speak up because no one will listen') and what we are compelled to do ('Other people should always come first'). They strongly influence our behaviour. They tend to 'leak' from some of the words and phrases we use: 'I'm only a secretary'; 'You can't leave people on their own for two minutes...' Other books on assertiveness go into this in more detail, and it is sufficient to say here that you may need to challenge your personally held beliefs from time to time.

Body language, or non-verbal communication, is particularly important when trying to communicate assertively. Consider the following:

▓ *Posture.* This should be relaxed but upright.

▓ *Appearance and clothes.* People will gain an impression from the way you look. Is this the impression you want to create?

▓ *Facial expression.* Frowns tend to be read in a negative way, even though you may be frowning as a result of concentration. Try to keep an open, friendly expression on your face.

▓ *Gestures and body movements.* Many of these are involuntary. Try to avoid distracting mannerisms.

▓ *Tone of voice.* This should be even and measured.

▓ *Gaze and eye contact.* Try to maintain a reasonable amount of eye contact with the people with whom you are communicating.

▓ *Non-verbal vocalisations.* This means 'hmm', 'I see', 'yes', 'uh-huh' and other sounds we make to show that we are listening.

Is your body language appropriate to the message you are trying to convey and the situation? The important thing is to ensure that there is congruence between what you say and how you say it. Remember what we said earlier about Professor Mehrabian's research; this means that if there is discrepancy people are more likely to take account of your body language than the words you use. Anxiety is likely to affect your behaviour, and may result in inappropriate body language, so learn one or two relaxation techniques. The following are easy to do, wherever you are, and have been found to be very helpful:

▓ Take two deep breaths, breathing from the diaphragm, and after each one let the breath out as slowly as possible, feeling the tension leave your body at the same time as the breath.

▓ Tense your muscles, then relax them and notice the difference. Become aware of any build-up of tension in your body. Be particularly aware of your jaw, neck and shoulders, as tension here can affect your voice.

practising assertiveness

General points to remember are:

■ Use a steady tone of voice, speaking clearly and not too fast. If your voice tends to crack or become strained when talking to others, practise some techniques to relax your jaw and shoulders.

■ Have a relaxed, but upright posture.

■ Try to avoid unnecessary padding, eg 'um', 'er', 'I wondered whether perhaps it might be possible for you at some stage to...?' (try 'Would you...?' instead). Keep 'I'm sorry' for the times you really do want to apologise and don't use it to plug gaps in the conversation or as a means of interrupting the other person.

■ If you don't understand something say so, and ask for clarification.

■ If you don't have the answer to a question, don't bluff but say so and offer to find out.

■ Remember that your behaviour will have an effect on the other person. If you yourself practise assertiveness you are more likely to get a positive response from others.

Strategies can help you to communicate assertively. Three of the simplest and most effective are:

■ *Basic assertion.* This is where you stand up for your rights in an assertive way, stating openly and honestly your feelings and needs. If you feel your assertive statement is being ignored or played down, or attempts are made to distract you, you should repeat it until such time as you feel you are being listened to and taken seriously. (This is sometimes called the broken record technique, based on the way the needle will stick on a scratch on a long-playing record and play the same short phrase of music over and over again.) Don't allow yourself to be side-tracked or drawn into an argument, but choose a form of words with which you feel comfortable, and keep on repeating the statement, for example:

- 'I am not prepared to rewrite the report to take account of your comments, which arrived after the agreed deadline.'
- 'My report is complete, and I am not prepared to rewrite it.'
- 'Please understand that I am not prepared to change my report.'

▓ *Empathy.* Many people feel unhappy with refusing a request in an assertive way, feeling that it somehow means they are rejecting the person. Using empathy softens the 'no'. It indicates to the other person that his or her request has been heard, and that the person making the refusal is sorry not to be able to comply. This approach is likely to defuse anger, as anger often arises because people feel they have been ignored. 'I realise that you are anxious for your comments to be included in the report. However, the deadline has passed, the report is now complete and I am not prepared to rewrite it.'

▓ *Workable compromise.* A compromise is acceptable if it seems likely to work well for each party. 'I am not prepared to rewrite my report to include your comments. However, I could arrange for them to be included as a late submission and tabled at the meeting.'

Here are some case studies for you to think about. Possible answers are given at the end of the section, but you will need to find an approach that works for you, and a form of words with which you are comfortable.

case studies

1. Your partner is going away on a conference and you have arranged for the children to stay with a friend. For the first time in years you will have the house to yourself for a weekend. You are treating yourself to a cup of coffee when the telephone rings. It is your mother, who wants to come and stay on that same weekend.

How do you handle it? Can you say no? If so, how?

2. Your boss asks you to stay late to complete an urgent report. S/he suggests that you go out for dinner together after the work is finished. You get on all right with your boss at work but you do not want to develop any kind of personal relationship.

What do you do?

3. You are having a drink in the pub with a friend. It's late and you're tired and ready to go home. You try to leave, but your friend insists on buying you another drink. You really do not want it.

What do you do?

How you respond to difficult situations will depend on a number of factors: how well you know the individuals concerned, what is the history of your relationship with them, whether you are in public or in private, how you are feeling that day, etc. I suggest that you identify situations in which you feel more, or less, comfortable, and those people with whom you are more, or less, able to be assertive. For example, some people find it easier to be assertive at work than at home, and with colleagues rather than family. For others it is the other way round. Once you've thought about this you will know which areas you need to concentrate on if you wish to improve your assertiveness skills.

Here are some suggestions for dealing with the case studies. When refusing invitations, try to say the word 'no' at an early stage, so that your refusal is quite clear. In all cases, try to avoid the little white lie, as invariably you will be caught out!

dealing with the case studies

1. Listen to how you feel. Are you really downhearted at the thought of having a visitor for the weekend, or is it a minor irritation? If the former, then you need to try to find a way to tell your mother that normally you love her company, you hate having to say no, but that it is really important to you to have some time to yourself. You could suggest another weekend or an alternative meeting – a shopping trip, perhaps.

Strategies: empathy, workable compromise, possibly broken record.

2. Be firm, but polite. Stay calm, and try to avoid either of you losing face. Ensure that your body language is appropriate – turn to your work and avoid holding eye contact. Bring the conversation back to the work you are doing.

Strategies: be firm and calm and match your body language to your words. Keep to the point; the broken record might be appropriate.

3. Stay friendly but be firm. Tell your friend that you hate to disappoint him or her, and that you look forward to a drink another evening. Then leave.

Strategies: empathy, workable compromise, body language. Don't hang around to be persuaded.

the telephone

introduction

Most homes have one. Every office does. A large proportion of
the population now carries a mobile version. They are to be
found on street corners, in railway stations, in shops, restau-
rants, factories, schools, theatres, pubs, clubs – the telephone is
ubiquitous.

Why do we make so much use of the telephone? Most
people would answer that it saves time. It is generally quicker
to ring someone up than to meet him or her face to face. If
it is quicker it is also likely to be cheaper. You can make
personal contact and get instant feedback, ie you can telephone
someone with an enquiry and get a response straight away.
Many important business deals are conducted on the telephone.

However, it can be intrusive. 'Cold calls' to private numbers
have to be handled sensitively to avoid causing annoyance. You
can control the calls you make but not the ones made to you.
Many managers would give the telephone as one of their major
time-wasters.

Using the telephone requires technical skills in the same way
as using a photocopier or a video player. However, unlike other

pieces of office equipment, interpersonal skills are also called for; it is these skills, so often neglected, that are the focus of this chapter.

the importance of the telephone

Telephones have been around since 1877 but it's fair to say that many of us still have a love–hate relationship with them. They seem to highlight and exaggerate any inadequacies we have in communicating with other people. You can't make up for the lack of the right word by your facial expression. You may wonder whether the other person is really listening. Sometimes your mind goes blank and you forget what you had to say. Ending telephone conversations politely but firmly is a problem for many people.

four good reasons why we use the telephone

With all these difficulties, why do we make so much use of the telephone? The first reason has to be *speed*. It is much quicker to pick up a receiver and dial a number than it is to dictate, write, or type a letter or e-mail. Even the time-wasting problem of finding that the number you want is busy, or not answering, can be helped if not altogether solved by the use of various facilities such as memories, last number redial and answering machines.

The second reason is *cost*. This may seem surprising at first when you look at the cost of telephone rental and calls. But in business you also need to take into account the cost and value to your company of your time and that of any staff working for you. You need to think of the time saved, which might give you just the edge you need over your competitors. When you take these factors into account the telephone is a very cost-effective means of communication.

Personal contact is the third reason. Although there is no visual contact you can hear a voice and build up a mental picture of the person. Even on the telephone it is possible to learn a great deal about how someone thinks, feels and behaves – and he or she can learn about you.

This leads on to the fourth reason, which is *feedback*. Unlike written communication, feedback via the telephone can be instant, and as we saw earlier it is feedback that turns a statement, or a question, into communication.

There are, of course, some occasions when it is better not to use the telephone, for example:

▧ it is usually better to talk through really difficult problems face to face as you can judge the other person's reactions and feelings better;

▧ it may be better to write to busy senior people;

▧ e-mail allows recipients to respond at a time that suits them;

▧ if a considered response is required;

▧ bad news may be better conveyed face to face, or by letter;

▧ if the information you wish to give is highly confidential;

▧ if a formal record is required;

▧ complex information is usually clearer when it is set out in writing;

▧ you may wish to avoid discussion with someone;

▧ cost may be a factor with long long-distance calls.

The telephone is a vital piece of equipment. Its importance can be demonstrated by thinking of the uses to which it can be put: selling, buying, explaining, information giving and receiving, discussing, negotiating, arranging, confirming, networking – the list is endless and these are just business calls! Even contracts and agreements may be agreed by telephone and confirmed later in writing.

---

case study

John, an architect, is sole proprietor of a design, advice and build company. He believes the telephone to be vital to his success:

> When the telephone stops ringing, I'm out of business. It complements face-to-face contacts with clients, subcontractors, suppliers, etc but it is not a substitute for this. It keeps things warm, but any business deals must be confirmed in writing. In face-to-face communication you rely heavily on facial expression etc, which is lost on the telephone, but you can cultivate the art of listening so that you can quickly pick up if someone is bored or frustrated – a sign that you are not getting through.

---

active listening

We have seen that feedback is an important feature of effective communication, and on the telephone, therefore, impact is potentially lost unless it is made up in other ways. Active listening is particularly important on the telephone. You cannot nod, smile, frown, etc, so you need to make a conscious effort to increase the number of times you say 'yes', 'Mm', 'I see', or even grunt; this indicates to the other person that you are paying attention. Ask questions, and constantly check for understanding. Say things like 'Am I right in thinking that you need more time before you can produce a final report?' or 'Are you saying that we should involve Personnel in our discussions?' At the end, summarise what you think has been agreed, and allow the other person time to respond: 'Are we agreed that I will brief the Chairman and you will write the report?'

On the telephone, all you have is your voice and it is important to make it sound clear, positive and interested. Accents are not important but clarity is. Sound enthusiastic – it may be difficult at the end of a long day, but it's worth it. Smile, and it will be heard. This may sound far-fetched, but there are both psychological and physiological reasons for the assertion. First of all, your spirits do rise when you smile. It is extremely difficult to continue to feel gloomy with a smile on your face. Secondly, the small muscles that lift the corners of the mouth also have an effect on the pitch of the voice, raising it a little and making it sound interested.

Above all, try to remain alert and interested. It is quite easy to tell when you have lost someone's attention, even on the other end of a telephone.

Practical points to watch out for are:

■ *Inflection.* Try not to talk in a monotone. Make your voice rise and fall.
■ *Tone.* This will reflect your attitude.
■ *Rate.* Don't speak too quickly. Give the caller time to take in what you have to say.
■ *Enunciation.* Speak clearly and never with something in your mouth (pipe smokers and pencil chewers, please note!). Be particularly careful with names of people, addresses, etc.

Here is an exercise to help you to think about how you deal with people on the telephone.

exercise – how do you behave on the telephone?

Each of the situations listed has three possible responses. Imagine yourself in each situation, and tick the response that is most like you:

A. A customer telephones, angry because of a delay to the delivery of his order. It is your job to deal with complaints but he insists on speaking to someone 'more senior'. You:

1. Get annoyed.
2. Apologise profusely because all the managers are out.
3. Explain that your job is to take down the facts and see if the problem can be resolved before referring it to a manager.

B. When you have a difficult call to make, do you:

1. Keep putting it off.
2. Plan what to say and how to say it, making the call at the first appropriate time.
3. Make the call when you feel in the mood without giving it any particular thought.

C. When people telephone to try to sell you something, do you:

1. Tell them to go away.
2. Allow yourself to be persuaded to meet them.
3. Say politely but firmly that you do not want the item.

D. A colleague whom you know well asks if you can help out with her workload. This has happened before. You say:

1. 'I'm fed up with this, Jane. It's not my job to help you out when you can't cope.'
2. 'Well, I don't know... oh, all right.'
3. 'No, Jane, I realise that you're busy. However, I can't help you this time as I have my own work to do.'

E. You need some figures at short notice for a meeting. You telephone the Finance Office and say:

1. 'I need information about travel costs for the Board meeting tomorrow. I'd be grateful if you could let me have these figures as a matter of urgency.'
2. 'I'm awfully sorry to bother you but I just wondered – er – could you possibly let me have the figures on – um – travel

costs some time – well, it's not really urgent but if you could let me have them by this afternoon...'
3. 'Look, you're going to have to drop everything and get me these figures now.'

F. The Managing Director telephones. You:

1. Panic.
2. Think 'I'm as good as he is any day.'
3. Deal with him efficiently and politely.

G. In the course of conversation someone criticises your boss. You don't agree. You say:

1. 'Well, I see what you mean.'
2. 'I don't think that's fair. I get on with her very well.'
3. 'You're just stupid and prejudiced.'

H. You have to tell a senior manager that the course he wanted to attend is fully booked. You:

1. Spend five minutes apologising before getting to the point.
2. Announce the news abruptly and anticipate possible criticism by saying, 'It's not my fault, they didn't tell me the closing date.'
3. Explain that the present course is full but the organisers hope to repeat it next year.

I. The telephone rings while you are talking to a visitor. You answer it and:

1. Try to hold two conversations at once.
2. Say 'I'm busy, you'll have to ring back.'
3. Explain that you have a visitor and ask if you can ring back, giving an anticipated time.

Key: If you ticked A3, B2, C3, D3, E1, F3, G2, H3, I3, you have behaved in a professional, assertive manner. You state your opinion calmly and firmly, whilst acknowledging the other person's point of view.

If you ticked A1, B3, C1, D1, E3, F2, G3, H2, I2, you tend to behave aggressively. You allow emotions to get in the way of clear communication, and have little regard for others' feelings or points of view.

If you ticked A2, B1, C2, D2, E2, F1, G1, H1, I1, you are unassertive and rather passive. You tend to let other people walk over you and have difficulty getting them to acknowledge your rights and opinions.

dos and don'ts

Let's start with the don'ts – 10 common ways to upset your clients.

1. Try not to sound *abrupt*. No matter how busy you are, when you pick up the telephone you are committed to the call, and must give it your full attention.
2. People at work are much less formal these days. However, this does not mean being *casual*. Your aim should be to sound both professional and friendly.
3. Saying '*hello*' and nothing else when you answer the telephone is unhelpful and can lead to confusion. Consider the following typical conversation:

'Hello.'
'Hello, is that Brooks Limited?'
'That's right.'
'I want the sales department.'
'Yes.'
'Sorry?'
'This is the sales department.'
'I need to speak to Peter Brown.'
'That's me.'
'Well, why didn't you say so in the first place?'

Would it not have saved time and frustration to say 'Good morning, Brooks Sales Department, Peter Brown speaking'? This is such a common problem that it is worth discussing it in some detail. Help your caller by saying, at the very least, 'Good morning/afternoon', and your name. This may be all that is needed if yours is a small organisation, or if the call is an internal one or has come through the switchboard, but if external calls come direct to you, you will need to give more information. It is best to say 'Good morning/afternoon' first, as this gives callers time to adjust their hearing to the sound of your voice. It also allows for any slight delay in connecting your call.

4.   Try not to *delay* in answering a call. This may be a problem for busy managers. However, it is a great irritation for people if their call is ignored or only answered after a long delay. Telephones should be answered within three or four rings. If you have a piece of work you simply must finish, or a visitor you need to spend time with, there are three things you can do:
     − Divert your calls to a secretary or colleague.
     − Advise switchboard that you are unable to take any calls.
     − Use an answering machine or voice mail.

5.   If you are in a *hurry* to be somewhere else, try not to sound impatient. Say something like 'I'm afraid I can't give this sufficient attention now as I have a meeting to attend. May I think it over and call you back tomorrow?' If you use this method, agree a convenient time for calling back − and don't forget to do so!

6.   Avoid jargon. *The Shorter Oxford Dictionary* defines jargon as 'the terminology of a science or art, or the cant of a class, sect, trade, or profession'. It is accept-

able to use jargon among members of the same profession, but it should only be used if you are sure it will be understood by the other person. Don't assume this, however. If in doubt, miss it out.

7. Do not imagine that by placing your hand over the mouthpiece you can prevent the caller from *hearing* what you are saying. Modern handsets contain a chip that means that the whole shell acts as a pick up. Your telephone may have a 'hold' or secrecy facility, but it is safest not to say anything you do not wish the other person to hear while you are still connected.

8. Never try to speak with something in your *mouth*, whether this is a pen, cigarette, finger or sandwich! Not only does it sound rude, but it makes your speech indistinct.

9. Don't be embarrassed by *pauses*. People need thinking time and there are gaps in any conversation. Even though these gaps are more difficult to accept on the telephone because you cannot see the other person's face do not feel compelled to fill them with meaningless talk.

10. Don't try to talk to *two* people at once.

getting it right – 10 steps to success on the telephone

making calls

1. Getting your call in *first* will help you to stay in control.

2. *Plan your calls.* Work out beforehand what you want to say, who you want to say it to, and your objectives – what you hope to achieve by the call. Anticipate further questions and have any relevant information in front of you when you telephone.

3. *Ask clearly* for the person you want and the department. Use the extension number if you know it. (Make a note to include your extension number on correspondence.) If secretaries ask for the *purpose* of your call, tell them (unless, of course, it is truly confidential). Secretaries these days are often regarded as members of the management team, and may well be the most appropriate people to deal with in the first instance.

4. When you get through, state *clearly* who you are and the reason for your call. Be as clear and concise as possible.

5. If what you have to say is long or confidential, it might be a good idea to *check* with the person you are calling whether it is a convenient time to discuss it.

receiving calls

6. *Smile* when you answer the telephone.

7. The exact form of *greeting* may be determined by policy, the size of your organisation and its relation to the switchboard, etc, but you should always sound lively and interested in what the caller has to say. Don't just say 'Yes' or 'Hello'. Do say 'Good morning' or 'Good afternoon', do identify yourself and/or your department and, if you want to sound really helpful, add 'How may I help you?'

use of names

8. Many companies encourage staff to use their customers' *names* as much as possible to increase the feeling of intimacy and friendliness. Learn as much as you can about regular customers and show interest in them. I would, however, add a word of warning: many people, especially older people, do not like to be addressed by their first name too early

in the conversation. Until you know people it is best to err on the side of formality. 'I'll check that for you, Mr Green' or 'Ms Jones, I'm so pleased you called' sounds polite and friendly. If you are taking down someone's name and address, ask yourself if it is really necessary to know whether a woman is married or not. 'Ms' is a convenient term that can be applied to all women.

ending calls
9. Sometimes people have difficulty *finishing* a call. Be assertive about it. Try one of the following phrases:
   - 'Thank you for your time. I know how busy you are so I won't keep you any longer.'
   - 'It's been nice talking to you. I'll be in touch again next week.'
   - 'I'll write to confirm our agreement; you should get the letter next week.'
   - 'I'll call again when I have had time to think about this.'
   - 'I have appreciated the opportunity to talk to you, Mr Green.' (The use of their names will usually attract the attention of verbose people.)
   - 'White' lies are not normally to be recommended, but if you are really hard-pressed you could try 'I'm sorry, I'm wanted on the other phone/there's a visitor waiting to see me.'
10. We tend to remember best things that are said at the start and the end of conversations, so it is a good plan to repeat back the gist of the conversation, and *summarise* any arrangements made. Use phrases like 'As I understand it...' or 'I think we agreed that...' Make it clear how matters are left.

special areas

transferring calls

The first tip is to get to know your system so that you can transfer calls quickly and efficiently. The second is to remember that being transferred can be very frustrating for the caller, so do keep the person informed about what is going on. Try the following steps:

▦ Explain to the caller what you are doing.

▦ Before putting the call through check with the recipient whether or not he or she can help.

▦ If there is a delay, return to the caller to explain and ask if he or she wishes to continue holding.

▦ If there is a real problem, ask if you can have the caller rung back when you have found someone to help.

▦ When you return to a caller who has been waiting, check whether he or she is still there before transferring.

messages

giving messages

▦ Always allow time for the other person to write the message down, pausing after each phrase.

▦ When dictating names or numbers, pause after meaningful groups of numbers or letters, eg 0207/333/1234 or H-a-z-e-l/t-r-e-e/L-a-n-e/, G-u-i-l-d-f-o-r-d,/ S-u-r-r-e-y.

▦ Check that the other person has taken the message correctly.

receiving messages

▦ Always write messages down as soon as you can. Try to keep a separate pad just for messages, rather than scraps of paper and used envelopes. Specially printed message pads are a good idea.

▨ Do not hesitate to ask for the message to be repeated, or for unfamiliar words to be spelt out.

▨ Read back the message to check that it is correct.

dealing with difficult situations

Overall, the best advice is: stay in control of your emotions. Never telephone when you are feeling angry. It is also a good tip to make the call, rather than waiting to be called – that way you have a better chance of staying in control. And make difficult calls early in the day, so that worrying about them won't get in the way of everything else you have to do.

The other person may also be experiencing anxiety. Your organisation may be very familiar to you but can seem large and frightening to someone calling from outside (and tension can make nervousness sound like aggression in some people). If you are friendly and helpful and patient, you will encourage the other person to relax and say what he or she has to say more clearly.

Don't forget to listen to the tone of voice for hidden messages – for example, someone saying 'I understand' in a very hesitant way may in fact be saying 'I don't know if I do understand'!

Make notes of important, difficult telephone conversations.

making a complaint

▨ Before you make the call, decide on your objectives. What do you hope to get out of making the complaint? A hearing, an apology, action, an opportunity to get something off your chest? What are you prepared to settle for?

▨ Marshal your facts and decide on strategy. Be careful in your choice of words.

▨ Practise the broken record technique (see Chapter 1).

receiving complaints

▧ Stop whatever you are doing and give the caller your full attention.

▧ Let the caller feel that he or she is being taken seriously.

▧ Listen to what is being said, concentrating on the facts rather than the emotions, and write the facts down.

▧ Allow the caller to have his or her say. Don't interrupt too soon.

▧ Show empathy (see Chapter 1) and apologise for any mistake that may have been made. Try to avoid apologising for something that is not your fault, and equally avoid putting the blame on someone else, the system, or the complainer. Don't agree with wild statements but say something like 'I can understand why you feel that way.'

▧ Don't make rash promises, and keep any promises you do make. Deal with the matter quickly.

▧ Keep the complainer informed of progress if this seems to be slow.

▧ If the complaint is justified, ensure that the same mistake does not occur again.

aggression

▧ Keep calm and try not to be drawn into an emotional state yourself, as this will only escalate the problem. Listen to the facts.

▧ Don't interrupt too soon but allow the person to let off steam.

▧ Recognise the person's anger and show understanding of its cause, but don't be drawn into making promises that cannot be kept, or giving ultimately unhelpful alternative suggestions.

▧ If the answer is no, say so and keep on saying so, calmly and reasonably. Try not to be drawn into an argument.

▨ You may well feel upset after a difficult telephone call, so try to find someone to talk to, or have a few minutes' break to allow your emotions to settle down.

requests for confidential information

▨ Confidential information should never be given out over the telephone as you have no proof of the caller's identity.

▨ The normal procedure would be to ask for the request to be made in writing. If the matter is urgent (eg the police) ask if you or the individual concerned can phone back.

▨ The 1984 and 1998 Data Protection Acts rule that personal information should not be disclosed either orally or in writing or accidentally to an unauthorised third party. Check further details with your Data Protection Officer.

▨ Learn to say no, politely but firmly.

case study

Jennifer is Research Manager of a large public sector organisation.

When I have to deal with difficult calls I try to prepare but I don't over-rehearse because you can be thrown if the other person says something unexpected. I start by asking how I can help or saying I understand the caller has a problem, and perhaps we can discuss this. A pleasant opening sometimes diffuses any anger. I make the assumption that most people given a chance would like to deal with problems in a civilised way. You have to try to judge how the other person is responding, and you only have the tone of voice to go by. If the caller is in an emotional state I will usually suggest I call back when the person has had time to calm down.

If you think someone wants to have a row with you it can give you a slight edge if you get your call in first. The most difficult calls are if we have made a mistake. I try not to put them off for too long. If I try to ignore them they keep niggling away at me.

using answerphones and voice mail

Answering machines are now so common that there can be very few people who have not encountered one. This does not mean, however, that they are universally popular. Here are some suggestions for making effective use of answering machines:

- Leave a friendly, non-threatening message on your own machine. Say who you are, apologise for not being available and encourage the caller to leave a brief message: 'Please leave your name and telephone number and we will call you back as soon as possible.' If there is a time limit on messages, say so. It is also a good idea to ask people to give the date and time of their call.
- Don't forget to phone back.
- If you encounter someone else's machine, don't panic. The outgoing message gives you time to clear your thoughts. Don't attempt to give a long message – your name, number, date and time of call, and a brief account of the reason for the call are sufficient. Say goodbye if you would otherwise feel uncomfortable, but it is not necessary. Treat the answering machine as a verbal message pad.

training your staff

All managers have a responsibility for the training and development of their staff. Even managers who work in large organisations with well-resourced training units should be prepared to monitor training needs and discuss with members of staff the purposes of any training that might be organised for them.

case study

Jennifer: As a manager it is important that if I get people to ring up on my behalf then they are speaking for me so I want to make sure that this is handled in a proper manner because it is saying something about me – it's equivalent to someone signing a letter on your behalf – you want to make sure that this is spelt correctly, but you don't want to have to check it every time. It is saying something about you and your management ability so it is important to me that the people ringing the office get an impression of courtesy and helpfulness and efficiency.

First of all, of course, it is important to use the telephone courteously and effectively yourself. It is no good instilling good practice into your sales team if you continue to snatch up the receiver and bark 'Yes!' into it yourself!

First impressions are important, and do last. We have all encountered someone for the first time who sounded bad-tempered, or curt. However much the person improves on acquaintance, it is hard to forget all about that first encounter. The memory stays. And if the person doesn't get the chance to improve – if you never speak to him or her again – you will remember that bad-tempered person who upset you one morning. As the saying goes: 'You never get a second chance to make a first impression.'

Staff should be familiar with the telephone system and its facilities so that they are confident and comfortable while using it. Give new staff the opportunity to visit the switchboard and meet the operators (and, incidentally, make sure that the switchboard knows the names of new staff). Training may be carried out by the system provider, outside consultants or internal training staff.

Junior staff, especially secretarial and reception staff, may be the first point of contact after the switchboard for other staff or members of the public. They may have to deal with all sorts of problems and must decide whether to try to handle these themselves, or hand them on to someone else. They will need training activities designed to boost confidence and enhance interpersonal skills.

Sales staff will need additional training to help them deal with incoming calls and outgoing calls. Outgoing calls will include calls to existing customers, and 'cold calls'. Areas that should be covered include:

▓ gaining confidence;
▓ planning and structuring a sales call;
▓ effective presentation of the product or service;
▓ listening, questioning and speaking;
▓ the art of friendly persuasion;
▓ closing the sale;
▓ follow-up calls.

summary

Key factors to ensure effective communication on the telephone:

▓ Be *clear*.
▓ Be *concise*.
▓ Be *courteous*.
▓ *Control* the call.

▓ Be *clear*:
  – speak clearly;
  – avoid jargon;
  – make sure you understand and are understood by giving and asking for feedback.
▓ Be *concise*:

- set objectives for each call;
- know who you want to speak to;
- know what you want to say;
- have any information by you as you make your call.
▓ Be *courteous*:
- don't telephone if you are angry;
- don't allow your frustration to show in your voice;
- always be polite;
- use personal names when appropriate;
- listen to the other person's tone of voice for hidden meanings;
- smile.
▓ *Control* the call:
- by planning;
- by practising assertiveness skills.

effective writing

Writing remains a key skill for all managers. There is, however, evidence to suggest that many young people starting work in the 21st century do not have a confident grasp of the principles of grammar and good English. There is much debate about why this should be, but one reason is undoubtedly the development and increasing use of telecommunications and electronic means of communication. In earlier centuries written communication was the only way in which people at a distance could keep in touch with one another and they took pleasure in writing letters. This is no longer the case, but the importance of good writing remains.

Good, clear writing should be the aim of all managers, and it is important to have a flexible style that can be adapted to meet the needs of your readers. This chapter takes you through the key areas of clarity, grammar, presentation and getting started, but it is not a complete guide to written English, and can only highlight some common grammatical difficulties and general points of good practice. A reading list is provided (see Further Reading) if you wish to pursue this in more detail.

First of all, what are the aims of good writing? I consider them to be:

- ▓ to raise the quality;
- ▓ to reduce the quantity;
- ▓ to save the writer's time;
- ▓ to make the reader's task easier.

When you have read the rest of this chapter you may wish to argue that there is no saving of the writer's time. Indeed, Pliny the Younger, who was famous for his letters, once wrote: 'I am sorry this letter is so long. I did not have time to make it shorter.' But the time will be spent on thinking and planning, not on the physical process of writing. You will see what this means in due course.

The criterion for good English is: how well does it carry out its particular function? The first question to ask yourself, therefore, is: what is the function of this piece of writing? What is my purpose in writing it? Is it to inform, persuade, enquire, negotiate, describe, reassure, entertain? Then think about your audience – the person or people to whom you are writing. Is it a friend, your boss, colleagues in the same business, customers, or the public at large? Each will require a different approach, and a different style. But each will require clear expression and a sound grammatical structure.

Writing good English is not difficult. Most native English speakers are able to speak good English from an early age. However, things often go wrong in transferring the spoken word to the printed page. Sometimes it's a result of forgetting that writing is or can be a permanent record. Small mistakes that go unnoticed in speech become glaringly obvious in print. Sometimes, however, we try too hard and end up with stilted prose that is hard to read and impresses no one. Try to find a style that is natural and comfortable to use, and then be prepared to make it a little more or a little less formal, according to the circumstances.

clarity

Unless you are writing a novel or a poem, your readers are unlikely to be interested in the niceties of your style, as long as it is clear. Unclear writing obstructs and creates an obstacle between the sender of a message and the receiver. The following examples of unclear writing were winners in the Golden Bull awards for poor English awarded annually by the Plain English Campaign. (The Campaign's Web site is well worth a visit: www.plainenglish.co.uk.)

Strathclyde Joint Police Board were asked how much it cost the taxpayer to police a particular protest. A council report summed up their response:

> Strathclyde Joint Police Board have confirmed that costing out a specific police operation is an awkward exercise in accounting terms as well as being an artificial practice. Making reference to the costs of a single operation is essentially an exercise in a vacuum which would divorce from the reality of the strategic approach to policing operations throughout the entire police area. Therefore an actual figure was not provided.

(A letter of mitigation was received – this means that the writers have seen the error of their ways!)

Terms and conditions from computer firm Elonex plc:

> The Company shall not be liable for the cancellation by it of any order or any unfulfilled part thereof or for effecting partial delivery or performance if performance by the Company is prevented or delayed whether directly or indirectly by any cause whatsoever beyond the reasonable control of the Company whether such cause existed or was foreseeable at the date of acceptance of the Customer's order by the Company or not and without prejudice to the generality of the foregoing any cause shall be deemed to prevent, hinder or delay the Company if the Company is thereby prevented, hindered or delayed from fulfilling other commitments whether to the Customer or to third parties.

The Department for Trade and Industry, in the Employment Relations Act 1999 (Schedule 7, section 3 (1) (c)):

> a person carrying on an employment business shall not request or directly or indirectly receive any fee from a second person for providing services (whether by the provision of information or otherwise) for the purposes of finding or seeking to find a third person, with a view to the second person becoming employed by the first person and acting for and under the control of the third person.

(A letter of mitigation was received.)

Why do people write this way? There are a number of reasons. One is tradition – older people may have been taught to write this way at school, and some professions have a tradition of writing in a style that seems wordy and convoluted to laypeople. Another reason is the mistaken belief that long words and complex sentences are impressive. Sometimes the reason is laziness – people write as they think and don't bother to rework their writing. Occasionally people choose to write this way to hide something; I suspect that Elonex's customers would be concerned to see how little it was offering in terms of customer service!

However, these days your readers are likely to be busy people with overflowing in-trays. They will be looking for writing that gets to the point quickly and is presented clearly and succinctly, without being abrupt or offhand. The following guidelines are intended to help you to achieve this goal:

1. Decide on your *key point* or points and make sure that these are given as much impact as possible. The closer they are to the beginning of a sentence or paragraph, the greater the impact.
2. Prefer *clear, familiar words*, and try not to use a long word when you can say exactly the same thing with a short one. Of course this doesn't mean that you should never use long words, but try to find precisely the right

word for the job you wish it to do. Never be afraid to use a dictionary. Avoid words with low information content like 'basically', 'simply', 'mainly'. Choose your words with care, and give equal attention to the order of words in the sentence. What the following writer meant, and what he said, were rather different: 'I grew up longing to be an MP but I have always wanted to write very badly too.'

3. Keep *most sentences short and simple*, with an *average* of 15 to 20 words per sentence. Variety will add interest. Try to keep one major idea per sentence as this will avoid any ambiguity and misunderstanding. The longer the sentence the more likely you are to go wrong. If a sentence contains two major ideas and begins to get confusing cut it in two.

The following example, from a firm of estate agents, could be improved both grammatically and in terms of impact:

> Gordon and myself have noticed a cooling effect on the property market within Central London, properties are on the market for longer and buyers have more choice hence viewing more properties before committing themselves.
>
> If you are thinking of selling, or trying to sell unsuccessfully please call us to discuss how marketing your property with Davis Brown will secure a good sale price in a convenient timescale.

Suggested answer:

> My colleague Gordon and I have noticed a cooling effect on the property market in central London, with properties staying on the market for longer. This gives buyers more choice and the opportunity to view more properties before committing themselves.
>
> If you are thinking of selling, or trying to sell, call Davis Brown to discuss how we can help you to secure a good sale price in a convenient timescale.

The *Gunning fog index* was devised to check the *readability* of your writing. Use it to calculate the readability of some of the examples given above. (A readability index is now available on some word-processing applications.)

Step 1) Starting from the beginning of any sentence, count out a 100-word passage. The passage must end with a full stop, even if it means going slightly over or under 100 words.

Step 2) Count the number of sentences in the passage and divide it into the number of words to get an average sentence length.

Step 3) Go through the sample counting out the words with three or more syllables. Do not count:
– proper nouns;
– combinations of easy words like 'typewriter' or 'newsletter';
– verb forms that make three syllables with their endings, eg assessing.

Step 4) Add the average sentence length (step 2) to the total from step 3 and multiply by 0.4.

The aim for good readability is between 10 and 14. A score over 20 will cause serious difficulties for most people.

4. Sir Ernest Gowers said that the paragraph is essentially a unit of thought, not length, and therefore should contain only the material relevant to the main statement in that paragraph. However, by breaking up the page and creating white space, paragraphs will also contribute to the overall readability of your writing.

5. Avoid overuse of the passive voice, which is when the doer of the action becomes the object of the verb. Examples are:

Passive	Active
The ice-cream was eaten by the child.	The child ate the ice-cream.
The plans will be discussed	The committee will discuss the plans.

The *active voice* is much more direct and vigorous. The passive voice gives objectivity but can be vague, imprecise and confusing. The doer may not be mentioned at all. For example, 'The records must be updated every three months' does not tell you who is responsible for carrying out this action, and it is possible that the records will not be updated. It would be better to say: 'The supervisor (or Joe Smith) will update the records every three months.' However, there may be occasions when the passive voice is preferred, for example in the writing of scientific and technical papers.

6. Try to fit your writing to your *audience*. This means being adaptable and developing a flexible style. Keep asking yourself 'How best can I communicate with this individual, or this group?' Give particular thought to what your readers already know in order to determine how much information to include, and at what level, as well as the most appropriate style and language to use.

7. Be brief (without being curt) and *avoid unnecessary padding*. Try to avoid words and phrases like 'basically', 'simply', or 'in close proximity to', which pad out and slow down your writing, without adding anything to the content.

Example

Dear Sir
We are sending herewith our order no 679 for Steel Angles and

Channels, which we are urgently requiring in connection with an important contract. Delivery is of extreme importance and we should like to have the material in our Works by next weekend if possible.

Suggested answer

I enclose order no 679 for steel angles and channels. These are required urgently, and I should like them to be delivered to our works by next weekend, 25 February.

Readers want to get to the heart of your message as quickly as possible and although a little introduction may be courteous, don't allow this to interfere with the content.

8. English is a living language, and therefore changes; words acquire new meanings, new words are created and some rules of grammar are amended as a result of popular usage. An example of a change of meaning is the word 'presently'. In medieval times this meant 'now, at this time'. Today it means 'in a little while' or 'soon'. The Internet revolution has coined many new words, such as, well, 'Internet'. It is now acceptable to end a sentence with a preposition, and to use the plural pronoun in order to achieve gender-free language. Some writers are even suggesting that split infinitives ('to boldly go') should be accepted, and apostrophes eliminated, and it is possible that in a few years' time there will be further relaxation of current rules of grammar.

9. Beware of *jargon*, which has been defined as the misuse of technical language. Jargon is acceptable shorthand among colleagues working in the same area, but may not be understood by others. If you are in any doubt about this, avoid it. Try to make your writing fresh and interesting and your own, and avoid clichés,

which lose impact through overuse, and slang words, which date.

10. *Abbreviations* – the warning attached to the use of jargon applies here: don't assume that everyone knows what you mean. The general rule is to spell the words out in full the first time you use them, followed by the abbreviation in brackets, eg 'The Ministry of Defence (MoD) rewrote and redesigned one of its forms using plain English techniques.'

common grammatical errors

Test the effectiveness of your writing by doing the following quiz, which is based on common problems. Guidance is given in the section immediately following the quiz, and the answers are at the end of the chapter.

exercise – effective writing

1. Find a shorter or simpler word or phrase for:

   (a) accordingly
   (b) endeavour
   (c) concerning
   (d) dispatch
   (e) at the present time
   (f) in view of the fact that
   (g) in the near future
   (h) co-operate together
   (i) it consists essentially of two basic parts

2. Define the meanings of the following pairs:

   (a) less; fewer
   (b) alternately; alternatively

  (c) imply; infer
  (d) practice; practise
  (e) stationery; stationary

3. Try to correct these errors, which have appeared in the press recently:

  (a) 'Mr Squire and myself supported the all party campaign against closure.'
  (b) 'When we first arrived in England a colleague invited my young son and I to spend Christmas with his family.'
  (c) 'Like many scientists, Dr King was attracted first to chemistry. She points out that going to a girl's school was an advantage.'
  (d) 'Its a shame it's ball is lost.'
  (e) 'Crossing the line, the train struck him.'

4. Rearrange the following sentences so that each has one clear meaning:

  (a) A discussion was held on overtime working in the conference room.
  (b) The staff were trained well before the new system was started.

vocabulary

Just as *gravely* and *seriously* are similar in meaning, supply a comparable partner to:

  strict
  determined
  argument

Big is to *small*
  as profound is to   ＿＿＿＿＿＿＿
  as energetic is to   ＿＿＿＿＿＿＿
  as descend is to   ＿＿＿＿＿＿＿
  as conceal is to   ＿＿＿＿＿＿＿

Stale is to *bread*

as _____ is to butter

as _____ is to milk

guidelines on grammar

1. *Troubles with number*
   'The rule that a singular subject requires a singular verb, and a plural subject a plural verb, is an easy one to remember and generally to observe. But it is extraordinary how often this simple rule is transgressed, even by educated writers with some pretensions to a high standard of writing'(Gowers, 1986).

2. *Problems with pronouns*
   I, you, he, she, it, we and *they* should be used to denote the person(s) or thing(s) being or doing something – the subject (*he* is kind; *he* loves animals).
   Me, you, him, her, it, us and *them* should be used to denote the person(s) or thing(s) affected by the deed – the object (I saw *him*).
   Myself, yourself, etc should be used for emphasis (I saw it *myself*) or reflexively (the cat washes *itself*).
   Prepositions (*to, in, out, from,* etc) should be followed by the pronouns *me, you, him, her,* etc.

3. *Punctuation*
   Punctuation should be logical; it should cause readers to pause when the sense demands it, but not make them do so when it does not. Gowers recommends that you 'put in stops to help your readers to understand you'. Here is an example of a letter that would benefit from a few punctuation marks:

September 12, 2000

Our Ref PD 6 292 812

Dear Mr ——,
I am writing to you with reference to the damage to your Aluminium doors I understand that you did not wish for them to be replaced but instead have a cover strip fitted, we have the cover strip into stock and have tried to contact you so that we may visit you at your property to fit them, we have tried to contact you to arrange a fitting date but we have been unsuccessful please would you contact me at the depot on the above telephone number at your convenience, I look forward to hearing from you.
Yours Sincerely,
Mrs ——

The incorrect use of punctuation can cause real misunderstanding, on occasion. The following story was quoted in the press a few years ago:

Comma cost nurse's job
A comma cost a nurse, Mrs Angela Penfold, her job, an industrial tribunal ruled yesterday.

Mrs Penfold, aged 50, wrote to her health authority in Torbay, Devon to complain about her senior nurse at a health centre in Bovey Tracey.

She said in her letter 'I have come to the opinion Mrs Pepperell is out to make my life hell, so I give in my notice.' Because of the unintended comma, the health authority took the letter to be her resignation.

When the authority later refused to allow Mrs Penfold to withdraw the letter, it was effectively sacking her, the tribunal ruled.

Mrs Penfold, who agreed that the letter was worded badly, said: 'I cannot write letters and I did not word it right. I never intended to resign. I meant that she was trying to get me to hand in my notice.'

After deciding that Mrs Penfold of Fore Street, Torquay, did not mean to resign, the tribunal adjourned a hearing of unfair dismissal.

Incidentally, this article is a good example of the inverted pyramid structure (see below). *Apostrophes* cause particular difficulties. The rules are that apostrophes are used:

▓ to show that letters have been left out of words (it's = it is);
▓ to indicate the possessive case. The rules are:
 (i) Add 's to singular words (the Pope's visit).
 (ii) Add ' to plural words ending in s (Battersea Dogs' Home).
 (iii) Add 's to plural words not ending in s (a children's playground).
 (iv) Don't add apostrophes to *his, hers, its, ours, yours* or *theirs*.

4. *Perplexing participles*
If you start a sentence with a phrase containing a participle (*Left alone in the house, On driving into the park*) you should attach your opening phrase to the correct person or thing. If you were the person left alone or driving into the park, the main part of your sentence should start with 'I'. Some sentences may need quite a lot of alteration; for example by changing 'On driving into the park a deer ran across the road' to 'As I drove into the park a deer ran across the road.'

5. *Which and that*
That is used to introduce clauses that must be included in the whole sentence in order for it to read as you intend (restrictive clauses); *which* is used to introduce clauses that could be removed from the sentence without effect (non-restrictive clauses). For example,

compare 'All cars that are parked on double yellow lines will be towed away' with 'My car, which is parked on the road, is blue.'

6. *Gender*

 If the sex of the person is unknown, the difficulty is that English has no singular pronoun to denote common gender. The grammarians' recommendation, during the past two centuries, has been that he, (*him*, *his*) should be used. Popular usage, however, has for at least five centuries favoured the plural pronoun they (*them*, *their*).

 Many people regard it as inequitable that the masculine pronoun *he* should be used to include both sexes, and therefore prefer to use *they*. One can avoid the difficulty from time to time by writing *he or she* but this grows unwieldy with repetition.

 (Abridged from Dear, 1986)

You may be able to avoid the problem by changing the order of words in the sentence. If you cannot, and the sex of the person is known, use he (*him*, *his*) or *she* (*her*). If the sex is not known, then use the plural pronoun (*they*). 'Nobody would ever marry if they thought it over' (George Bernard Shaw, quoted in Dear, 1986).

avoiding discrimination

It is important to use language that is inclusive, and to be sensitive to the risk of patronising, offending or excluding colleagues or clients through your use of language. Here are some examples of alternative words and phrases that you might find useful:

Avoid	Prefer
affliction, handicap	impairment, condition, difficulty, disorder

best man for the job	best person for the job
Christian name	first name, forename, given name
cleaning lady	cleaner
half-caste	mixed race
man or mankind	humanity, human race
spastic	person with cerebral palsy
the disabled	disabled people or people with disabilities

organising writing

Most people who write have experienced writer's block, when it seems that they will never be able to get started. However, there are ways of overcoming this. Planning is essential, and so is the discipline to keep to your plan. Let's look at this in terms of *before*, *during* (the process of writing) and *after*.

before

Think about you, the *writer*. Why are you writing this? What is the purpose? What are your terms of reference? Who are your *readers* and what are their needs? How familiar are they with the subject? If you don't know, how are you going to find out? What *material* do you need, and where is it to be found? When is the *deadline*? How are you going to fit the writing into your overall *workload*?

How well do you manage your time? Are you a procrastinator, for example (many writers are)? Are you creative and imaginative in finding things to do that prevent you from sitting down at your desk and picking up your pen, or moving from the mouse to the keyboard? If you have serious problems you should turn to a course or book on time management (try M Haynes's *Make Every Minute Count*), but here are a few tips that might help you:

▒ Make an appointment with yourself, and write it in your diary. Block out a period of time and treat it as if your work were a visitor to ensure that there are no interruptions. Don't check your post, voice mail or e-mail until the allotted time is up.

▒ Tell yourself that writing can be enjoyable, and that it is deeply satisfying to create a good piece of work

▒ Promise yourself a treat when you have finished. This might simply be giving yourself a mental pat on the back, or telling a colleague about your success. Or make yourself a coffee or buy some flowers or a bottle of wine on the way home.

You then need to organise the time you have allocated for writing. How long is the piece of work to be? Can it be divided into sections to be worked on separately? Have you all the information you need, or do you need to do further research? Do you need to involve other people? What are their commitments?

I have two recommendations here: firstly, collect all the information before you start writing so that the flow of writing is not interrupted, and secondly, allow sufficient time for checking. Always have a break after writing and before checking.

writing

Getting started is a problem for many writers. The problem is caused by the creative processes of thinking and generating ideas becoming confused with the practicalities of writing clearly and grammatically in a suitable structure.

I am therefore going to suggest that you separate the two processes, and concentrate your energies on creating ideas before worrying about how you are going to express them. You may have come across *brainstorming* in another context. Brainstorming encourages creativity and the generation of ideas, and the crucial point is that you record *all* the ideas you have about a particular subject without stopping to evaluate them. You will need to write them down, because there is a limit to the number of ideas you can carry in your head at any one time. Only when you have finally exhausted your ideas do you begin to evaluate and delete those that do not seem relevant.

It is very important at this early stage to map out your ideas as a pattern, rather than a list down a vertical sheet of paper. If you write them as a list you are imposing a structural hierarchy on the writing at too early a stage. Once you have ideas numbered 1, 2, 3, etc, it is very hard to break away from this. I therefore recommend that you use a variation of brainstorming called *pattern notes*. To create pattern notes you need a large sheet of paper (A3 for preference and landscape rather than portrait format) and some coloured pens. In the centre of the paper write the title or topic of the paper you are writing. Around this central theme, write down all the ideas you have about it. Continue until you've exhausted your ideas. The coloured pens will help you to identify different strands to the theme. Add drawings and diagrams if it encourages your creativity. After that, you can evaluate and cross out those ideas that are irrelevant or inappropriate to this particular piece of writing. Then use your coloured pens to make links between ideas, so that you are beginning to work on the structure. An example of pattern notes is given in Figure 3.1.

The next step is to consider the *structure*. This should consist of related groups of ideas. Bear in mind the purpose of the writing, and the audience. Is your information going to be presented in chronological order? Will you work through the subject logically with your reader? Will you start with the big picture and fill in the detail or build up gradually? Once you have decided, write an *outline* with chapter or section headings

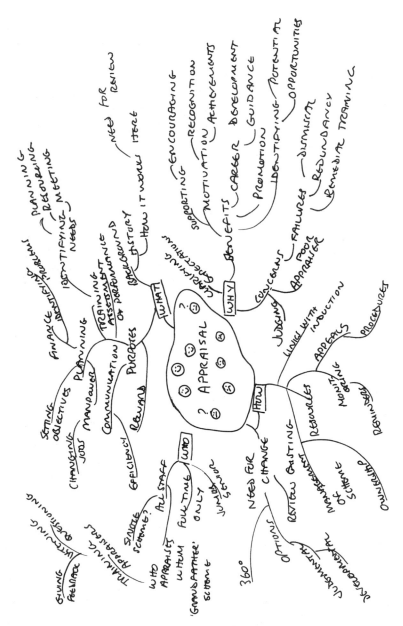

Figure 3.1 *Example of pattern notes*

and the main points to be covered in each section. Each section should have two or three key points, which should be easily identifiable.

As children, we are usually taught to write a piece of work with a beginning, a middle and an end. We are now going to consider an alternative structure, in which you start with your conclusion and then provide information to back it up. This is called the *inverted pyramid*, and it is how journalists are taught to write. Look at any newspaper and you will find examples of this.

'Local woman seriously ill in hospital' may be the heading. The next line reads: 'A local woman is in hospital with serious injuries after being knocked down by a bus in Maple Avenue on Friday night.' The rest of the article goes on to describe the woman, where she lives, how many children she has and what she was doing in Maple Avenue on Friday night. It might give the extent of her injuries and how long she is likely to be in hospital.

Journalists are recommended to start articles with the 'hidden' words, *I want to tell you that...* If you have these words in your mind at the beginning of a factual report or article, they will guide you into putting your message across most effectively.

There are many reasons for using the inverted pyramid structure. If you say at the start what is intended, you avoid misunderstandings. You control what your readers get out of your writing by declaring early what they should get out of it. Giving the conclusion at the start allows readers to decide whether or not they need to find out how you reached that conclusion. (However, although the conclusion comes at the start of the finished article or report, it is in fact almost the last thing you write.)

Now, at last, you are ready to write a first draft. You may find it helpful to use the document outline facility on your word-processing software. Bear in mind that this is only a first draft, and you must be prepared to revise and edit. This is the point at which you may wish to write the conclusion or summary. The next thing to consider is *presentation* – how the document will look on the printed page. It should look crisp, professional and easy on the eye. Choose a suitable typeface, and don't vary this too much – a variety of different typefaces and sizes looks untidy and can confuse. Decide on your hierarchy for headings and subheadings, ie capitals, underlined, italics. Make sure there is plenty of white space at the margins and between paragraphs. If you are using illustrations, try to ensure that these are as close as possible to the related text.

after

This may include typing if you prefer to draft by hand. In any case, the document will require careful checking followed by revision. Always have a break between writing and revising. We all have a tendency to read what we expect to read, and the fresher the piece of writing is in your mind, the more likely this is to happen. You need to read it as objectively as you can.

Editing is the key to good writing. Go through the document once, amend all the obvious errors, leave it for a while and then go through it again and be ruthless with the red pencil or the delete key. Longer documents may require three or four drafts.

Be hard on yourself. Cut out unnecessary words and phrases that do not contribute to the overall meaning; aim for clarity above all. Try to read it as your reader will.

If the document is long, don't always revise from page 1 and work through to the end. If you do this you will inevitably find that the later sections are less carefully revised, as you get tired. It is often the case that the early pages give the background, while the later ones develop the argument and therefore need to be written with particular care. Vary your approach by sometimes starting with the last section, and working backwards.

You may find it helpful to have a checklist so that you can go through the document systematically.

Revision has two aspects: structural and textual. Structural revision means looking at how the ideas flow and relate to one another in relation to the whole picture. Textual revision means looking at the grammar, spelling, vocabulary, paragraphs and sentences. Both are important. You may find that you need to print out your document, rather than reading it off the screen, which seems to take special skill. Despite new technology, this writer still finds herself spreading pages out on the floor, using coloured pens to indicate text that needs to be moved, and even cutting out sections and moving paragraphs around physically. For this reason you should never use both sides of the paper.

Finally, just before you send the document off, have one last check.

effective writing exercise – answers

1. Find a shorter or simpler word or phrase for:

		Suggested answers
(a)	accordingly	so
(b)	endeavour	try
(c)	concerning	about
(d)	dispatch	send
(e)	at the present time	now
(f)	in view of the fact that	as
(g)	in the near future	soon
(h)	co-operate together	co-operative
(i)	it consists essentially of two basic parts	it has two parts

2. Define the meanings of the following pairs:

(a) less; fewer	less applies to quantity, extent, degree; fewer to number
(b) alternately; alternatively	succeed in turn; one or the other
(c) imply; infer	hint; deduce, conclude
(d) practice; practise	noun; verb
(e) stationery; stationary	paper, pencils, etc; not moving

3. Try to correct these errors, which have appeared in the press recently:

   (a) 'Mr Squire and myself supported the all party campaign against closure.'
       Suggested answer: 'Mr Squire and I supported the all party campaign against closure.'
   (b) 'When we first arrived in England a colleague invited my young son and I to spend Christmas with his family.'
       Suggested answer: 'When we first arrived in England a colleague invited my young son and me to spend Christmas with his family.'
   (c) 'Like many scientists, Dr King was attracted first to chemistry. She points out that going to a girl's school was an advantage.'
       Suggested answer: 'Like many scientists, Dr King was attracted first to chemistry. She points out that going to a girls' school was an advantage.'
   (d) 'Its a shame it's ball is lost.'
       Suggested answer: 'It's a shame its ball is lost.'
   (e) 'Crossing the line, the train struck him.'
       Suggested answer: 'As he crossed the line, the train struck him.'

4. Rearrange the following sentences so that each has one clear meaning:

   (a) A discussion was held on overtime working in the conference room.

> *Suggested answer: A discussion on overtime working was held in the conference room.*
(b) The staff were trained well before the new system was started.
   Suggested answer: The staff were well trained before the new system was started.

vocabulary
Just as *gravely* and *seriously* are similar in meaning, supply a comparable partner to:

	Suggested answer
strict	firm
determined	resolute
argument	debate

Big is to *small*
   as profound is to *shallow*
   as energetic is to *lazy*
   as descend is to *ascend*
   as conceal is to *reveal*

Stale is to *bread*
   as *rancid* is to butter
   as *sour* is to milk

face-to-face communication

This chapter looks at those areas that affect all managers: communicating with your team, giving feedback, participating in and chairing meetings. More specialised areas such as selection interviewing, appraisal, counselling and disciplinary interviews need fuller coverage than can be provided here.

improving communication in your team

The fact that information can readily be communicated to your team via electronic means does not negate the need for meetings. Communication is generally most effective when people meet face to face, and you are more likely to get commitment and understanding when you know people as people rather than as e-mail addresses or disembodied voices. Debate, discussion, the generation and sharing of ideas, developing rapport, commitment to the task and to one another are all improved when people get together and can pick up and respond to the subtle cues that are so difficult to convey by e-mail or telephone.

working with your team

As a manager, your best results will come from the people you manage, which means putting effort and commitment into getting the best out of them. There are efficiency gains when work is properly distributed, there are clear objectives, responsibilities and tasks are delegated, and people work to their strengths and seek actively to reduce their weaknesses. There are psychological benefits to be gained from working with others, rather than in isolation, and a happy team is a productive team.

There is evidence that shared knowledge is often of higher quality and therefore greater benefit than ideas generated by one person alone, however creative that individual may be, and therefore team meetings are important. However, meetings take time, and time is money. How can the manager ensure that the time the team spends together is used most productively?

In order to encourage ideas from all of your team you need to build a positive atmosphere, bringing everyone into the discussion and encouraging participation. As team leader you will need to retain overall control in order to encourage people to see the broad picture before focusing on the detail, and to discourage over-hasty judgements and personal criticisms. The team needs to be encouraged to listen to and acknowledge one another's contributions; workplaces are competitive environments, and there is pressure on people to show off what they know and disparage other suggestions. However, disagreement can be creative and stimulating, and should not be discouraged, but rather used constructively. It helps if people can be prompted to separate opinion from fact and to be specific in their criticisms. The concept of devil's advocate is well known (this is someone who takes an opposing view for the sake of the argument). Less common is the idea of an angel's advocate, which involves thinking of positive aspects to an unpopular idea. This gives people the confidence to continue to put forward ideas, even though they may not be implemented.

You may have in your team people who react very quickly to ideas, and others who react very slowly, or not at all. Both can inhibit the generation of ideas. You will need to find a way to restrain the one and encourage the other (without putting the one down or the other on the spot). Quick reactors are often enthusiasts. They tend to have lots of ideas themselves and find it difficult to listen to other suggestions. Their comments may be unfocused and not thought through. They need to be encouraged to think before they speak, and to allow other people time to respond. Slow or low reactors may be negative or they may simply be quiet, but either way they tend to have a deadening effect on the team and its ability to generate ideas. They need to see that their contribution is important to the overall well-being of the team and the success of its task.

The technique of brainstorming, described in Chapter 3, might be useful in stimulating contributions. It should be used with problems that have been clearly identified and that will benefit from the combined creative energies of the team as a whole.

giving feedback

All managers should give feedback regularly and constructively to the team both as a group and as individuals. This is vital for the achievement of the team's work and for the development of individual members. Carried out in a constructive manner, feedback can help to solve problems, strengthen relationships, build trust, reduce stress, avoid conflict and help development.

You may be used to thinking in terms of praise and criticism. The word 'feedback' suggests a more constructive and focused response to performance. There are three types of feedback:

▦ *Motivational*, when you acknowledge what people are doing well; this motivates and increases confidence and encourages the repetition of behaviour that is valued. It is most beneficial when it is specific and related to observed behaviours or activities.

▦ *Formative*, when you encourage the individual to find different or better ways of performing a task or tasks; this increases competence.

▦ *Summative*, when you make a judgement about someone's performance or behaviour, based on objective criteria. This may form part of a test or examination, or appraisal, promotion, or disciplinary procedures.

In this chapter the emphasis is on giving formative feedback:

1. Formative feedback is best treated as a two-way, problem-solving process, and is therefore only useful if it deals with problems that can be solved. This means dealing with behaviour and facts, not personality and attitude. In order to be productive the person must:
   - understand the information;
   - be able to accept the information;
   - be able to use the information.
2. Try to separate facts from opinions. When giving your opinion, make it clear that this is what you are doing.
3. Try to be descriptive rather than evaluative: 'I found your voice a little quiet at times' rather than 'Nobody could hear you.'
4. Feedback should be in terms of specific, observable behaviour, not general or global. Try to avoid judgements such as 'good' or 'bad'.
5. Be timely. All types of feedback should be given as close as possible to the event that has given rise to the need for feedback. Choose an appropriate time and place.
6. Be prepared – plan your approach. Gather any infor-

mation or evidence that you need in advance, and think about your bottom line. What outcome are you hoping for – an apology, an assurance that it won't happen again, a longer-term change in behaviour? Decide in advance what you will settle for.

7. Be positive – show confidence that the problem can be solved.
8. Listen carefully. Check that you both understand each other.
9. Get commitment on action to be taken, if appropriate, and agree some form of follow-up.

coaching

Coaching has only recently become recognised as a valid management activity. Prior to this, the term was used to describe a process of preparing individual students for an examination, or an athletic or sporting contest. However, over the past 20 years or so it has been taken up enthusiastically by all those interested in developing people, and many organisations now incorporate coaching as part of their human resource strategy. So what actually is coaching? It is a means of helping individuals to maintain and improve performance, and at its most effective will encourage both professional and personal development. It fills the gap between what may be learnt on a formal 'off the job' course, and the job itself. It is usually job-specific and based in practice. It relies on accurate and impartial observation by the coach. Although special coaching sessions may be arranged, the skilled coach finds opportunities to coach in the normal course of events, for example when delegating or problem solving. There are links with appraisal, when formal objectives may be agreed; coaching helps the individual achieve those objectives.

The aim is to help people to work out the solution for themselves, set their own goals and learn from both successes and failures. The process can also be used to give insights into the coach's job in order to help the individual's understanding and development. For example, a coach could take the opportunity to talk through major events, such as the annual presentation to the Board, meeting a major new client, or preparing for a quality audit. Ideally time would be found before the event to talk through the implications and alternative approaches, and time afterwards to review what happened and what might be learnt from the event. The coach's overall attitude should be 'What can we learn from this?'

Teams can be coached as well as individuals; in this case the coach's aim is to harmonise individual effort to achieve cohesive team performance, and an understanding of group dynamics is important for those who coach teams.

A good coach needs to have skills and practical experience in the job, the ability to analyse performance, and strong interpersonal skills – active listening, questioning, giving feedback, developing rapport and trust, and raising self-awareness. Questions should be used to trigger reflection and analysis, to challenge assumptions and search for alternatives. Examples might be 'What did you take into account when making this decision?', 'What else might you have done?' and 'What were the alternatives?'

The experienced coach will take into consideration the individual's preferred learning style: whether this is an activist who learns best from practical experience; a reflector who prefers to observe and reflect before acting; a theorist who likes to organise observations and experiences into systems and theories; or a pragmatist who likes to test out theories to see which works best (see Honey and Mumford, 1983). Your own style will need to take account of the individual's experience and existing skills; the more experienced the individual, the less instructional and 'hands on' you should be.

Timing is important. Feedback is most effective when it follows soon after the behaviour on which you want to comment; on the other hand it is important to allow some time for the individual to reflect. Nobody likes failure and people may react emotionally and illogically to criticism, so this must be given in a context of support and encouragement.

dealing with conflict

Managers need to accept that a certain amount of conflict is inevitable when people work together and that you are unlikely to be able to eliminate it altogether. Rather, you should seek to identify and minimise unhealthy conflict, that is, conflict that seriously affects individual and team morale, and achievement of the task.

Open communication, consultation, a collaborative approach towards management and a belief in the values of teamwork are all important if you wish to avoid unhealthy conflict, but most important of all is seeking a win-win, rather than win-lose, solution, whatever the disagreement, thereby avoiding loss of face and loss of self-respect.

The symptoms of conflict are usually evident: rows, lack of communication, complaints, expressions of frustration, low morale, absenteeism, the development of a 'blame' culture. The causes may be interpersonal hostilities (people simply not getting on together as a result of personal differences); competition; role confusion; different objectives and values; and problems relating to territory (overcrowding, intruding on personal space, etc).

If addressed at an early stage, it may be possible to turn incipient conflict into more productive competition. You need to take action before positions get entrenched, and before loss of face becomes a major issue. The following are necessary:

■ The group is clear about its overall objectives.
■ There is acceptance that there may be more than one way of achieving these objectives.

▧ There is information available about progress towards objectives.

▧ It is accepted that mistakes may be made and failure is not a crime.

▧ Basic human rights are respected (for example, the right to be listened to and taken seriously).

If these are all in place there is a good chance that competition will not deteriorate into conflict, and there is much that you can do in building your team to ensure that they stay in place.

If there is real conflict there are strategies for dealing with it, which may be short-, medium- or long-term. None will guarantee success, and they will be affected by your personal style – are you assertive, aggressive or passive? Do you usually confront issues head on, avoid them, or try to find a compromise? You need to be aware of your preferred approach, and be prepared to adapt according to the situation.

Talking things through in order to make sure that you thoroughly understand the problem and its causes should be your first step. Is there any common ground that might provide an opportunity for joint problem solving? Ensure that all parties understand the difficulties that the conflict is causing, without allocating blame to anyone.

Short-term solutions may solve the immediate problem, thus buying you time, but could result in trouble being stored up for the future. Examples include smoothing things over, 'buying someone off' by offering an alternative to the thing he or she really wants, getting agreement to a compromise, or procrastinating in the hope that the problem will go away. Medium-term solutions include rearranging offices so that antagonists are kept apart, using your authority to force a solution, bringing in another person to arbitrate, mediate or counsel, or in some way amending the rules of the game so that everyone has something to gain. Finally, you might have to consider reorganising work so that antagonists work in different teams, on different shifts, or on different projects; not only will this keep them apart but it will distract attention from the conflict by giving them something else to think about. If all else fails then you might have to turn to formal procedures.

meetings

Meetings are an important feature of working life in most organisations, and research suggests that managers spend about 60 per cent of their time in meetings. They can serve a variety of purposes including decision making, team briefing, information exchange, consultation, negotiation, problem solving. Individuals can do a great deal to ensure that the meetings they attend are effective and productive rather than time-consuming and non-productive.

Sue is a senior manager who enjoys meetings. She believes that there is plenty you can do to help make meetings effective, even when you are not in the chair:

■ Understand the purpose of the meeting.
■ Understand your role and what is expected of you.
■ Do your homework. Read the papers in advance, mark them up and think about the interventions you wish to make. You may wish to consult with people who see you as their representative at the meeting, or with key people whose support you need.
■ If you have been invited to a meeting it's because you have something to contribute so don't be afraid to voice your opinion.
■ Be facilitative and remain committed to a positive outcome. If you disagree with what someone says do so as constructively as possible, acknowledging what was good in the suggestion before giving your own view. Avoid interrupting or contradicting the person outright.

Other practical things to help the meeting along include arriving on time, paying attention, asking questions, supporting useful ideas, taking notes and being prepared to take actions. You could make suggestions assertively – 'Would it be useful if…?' or 'I'd find it helpful if…' You might create space for people who find it difficult to bring things up by saying 'I think X has done some work on this', or indicating to the chair that you think Y has something to say. It's important to be open and inclusive in everything you do rather than closed and excluding.

Sue suggests:

> Watch your fellow members as well as listen to them. There is often much more information available about what's going on by watching people than by what they say. Meetings are like directing a play; they are about exits and entrances, and nuances, and subtleties of plot. I never understand why people say they are bored at meetings.

She also recommends that you should:

> watch people who operate effectively in meetings. It's like tennis – you can't learn it by reading a book. You can read a book, but then you have to go out and practise.

If you are new to the meeting you may prefer to limit your contribution but if there is a suitable opportunity explain that this is because it is your first meeting. You can show by your body language that you are interested in everything that is going on. You might find it useful to visit the room where the meeting is to be held in advance, and perhaps try out your voice. Where you sit is important, so if you have a choice try to choose a spot where you can catch the chair's eye and also see other members. Some rooms have 'dead spaces' so avoid these if you can. Sue also says:

> If you are a woman, it's a good idea not to sit near the teacups. It sounds silly but don't allow yourself to get in a situation where you feel you've got to behave in a way that you're not very comfortable with.

Afterwards, reflect upon what happened. Overall did you feel comfortable or uncomfortable? What made you feel that way? Did you feel that you had any influence over the discussion and contributed to the decision taking? If not, why not? Is there anything you can do about it next time? Take time to reflect, and if things didn't go well, be prepared to try a different approach next time. Don't forget, however, that reflecting on what does go well is also important.

chairing meetings

Isobel has chaired meetings of voluntary groups for a number of years. She thinks that the most important characteristics of a successful chair are commitment, respecting people's opinions, encouraging contributions from everyone, discouraging domination by one or two members, not dominating yourself, keeping an open mind, preparation and keeping to time.

> The first thing a chair has to be is very aware of the background and the history of the group that he or she is chairing, so therefore I've always tried to go through the background minutes, try to find out a little bit about the group, what makes them tick, what upsets them, what doesn't upset them, etc.

It's good practice to ensure that meetings start on time, and to set a finish time. If someone with an important contribution to make has to leave early you can suggest that the order of the agenda is amended to take account of this.

> I always try to set time boundaries and say we will stop at 4 pm so there isn't this tendency to go on and on so that people get fidgety and it all gets a bit boring.

Good chairs practise general listening, observing, questioning and summarising skills. They need to be aware of the content of the meeting, its structure, and the interaction between members, and between members and the chair.

You need to understand enough of the *content* to recognise what the priorities are, and to know who has particular knowledge or expertise. Arrange to be briefed beforehand if necessary. If the group includes experts, make sure that everyone understands their role and whether they are to be included in the decision-making process. If the discussion moves into an area you don't understand, or have insufficient knowledge of, it's best to be honest and admit this. Isobel says:

> I think it's vital that the chair doesn't appear to be a know-all but is willing to say "I don't know anything about this but I'm willing to investigate it if we can put it on to the next agenda."

The agenda provides a *structure* for the meeting, and it is important that the chair and the secretary work closely on this. Important items should be early enough in the agenda to allow sufficient time for discussion. Time management is important, and you might consider allocating times to the various items, to ensure that you cover 'for information' items quickly and allow sufficient time for discussion of the items that have been identified in the agenda as 'for consideration'.

Isobel says:

> Keeping it going and not getting bogged down on one subject is important, which means saying "We've spent 20 minutes on this; can we get some consensus of opinion now?" or "Can we reach a decision now or should it be put off to the next meeting while you think about it?"

Committee procedures are there to help both structure and process, for example keeping to the agenda, and addressing questions and comments to the chair. If you are responsible for a series of regular meetings you may find it helpful to agree rules about, for example, the length of the meeting, the order of items, whether to allow substitutes and how to deal with confidential or sensitive material.

Inexperienced chairs sometimes concentrate on the content, rely on the secretary for the structure and neglect the *interac-*

tion. However, if this is poor the meeting may be a waste of time. As Sue says:

> When meetings are chaired well it's satisfying but if the meeting is not getting more than the sum of the individual contributions it's not worth having.

New members should be properly inducted into the committee so that they understand the purpose and any rules and procedures. At their first meeting they should be introduced to the other members.

Encouraging contributions from all members of the group is not always straightforward and requires high-level interpersonal skills, as we shall see. A common difficulty is what to do about people who are talkative and dominate every meeting. It's a familiar problem to Isobel:

> In my experience there is nearly always somebody at any meeting who will try to monopolise everything and I think that's one of the skills that you learn or are sensitive to over a period of time. On the whole you have to give them the opportunity to say their say but then not allow them to monopolise the whole meeting.
>
> I think the role of a chair is in a sense a guiding role: to see that we get through the agenda, to allow everybody to contribute, to try to hold back those who contribute too much and to encourage those who don't contribute and don't ever say anything, by asking once in a while 'What do you think?' and 'Tell us what you think.' You need to be not impartial exactly but not to put your opinions over and above everybody else. If you come across something you don't agree with, don't say 'I don't agree with any of that' but say 'Any other opinions?' and try to move people round, or maybe put in something like 'Yes, but if we go in that direction bear in mind...' or 'It might be xyz when it would be better to be abc.'

Isobel remembers one particularly dominant person, who had lots of good ideas but her monopoly of the discussion meant that other people were inhibited from contributing. In the end the person who was chairing suggested that the two of them met separately, outside the meeting, in order to give her suggestions proper consideration, after which a report was prepared for the committee to discuss. This had a successful outcome – the dominant person felt that her contributions were appreciated, and the rest of the group were able to respond to the written document.

This sounds fine in principle but how do you intervene without being rude? It's important to try to find a pause and be prepared to step in quickly to say something like 'That was very interesting, Peter; now I'd like to hear from someone else' or 'That was a helpful contribution, Anne; what do other people think?' The conscious use of body language can help, such as a discouraging hand gesture and avoiding eye contact.

Occasionally you run into difficulties when the whole group is silent. Check the body language to see if it gives you any clues about whether this is because they are thinking over some difficult issues, or because they are uninterested. If the former, ask if anything needs clarification and then be patient and wait for a response. If time is pressing you could suggest holding the item over until next time to allow more time for consideration. If the group seems to have lost interest try having a break for tea, or suggest that you come back to it later and move on to the next item. Make sure that you yourself sound lively and interested and consider taking a different approach, perhaps using visual aids if they are available, or considering things from a different perspective.

You may have heard of the 'mouse at the meeting' theory. This holds that if someone doesn't speak for the first 10 minutes of a meeting, they are unlikely to talk at all! Therefore, try to get everyone to say something early in the meeting; if there are newcomers you could ask everyone to introduce themselves.

If there are conversations between two members of the group that don't include the others there are one or two strategies you could try:

■ Be silent yourself and look at them until they stop.

▓ Intervene and ask what they wish to contribute.

▓ Say 'I will continue with the agenda when everyone is ready.'

Some people are over-interested in the fine points of the issue being discussed. Their points may be valid but can hold up the discussion and can affect the motivation of the rest of the group. You need to find a way to acknowledge their contribution by saying something like 'These details need to be considered before implementing the scheme, but first of all I'd like to reach agreement in principle.' You might then ask those concerned with the details to take on a special role checking them after the meeting.

Occasionally people may be hostile; either to you, to other people in the group, to particular items on the agenda, or to the overall purpose of the committee or meeting. If you are faced with this, try to identify the cause of the antagonism as this will help you to know how to deal with the situation. Generally be firm but non-confrontational, ask the individual to explain his or her opposition and if this is more than an isolated occurrence you may need to arrange a separate one-to-one meeting.

negotiation

As with other forms of communication, it helps to prepare carefully before a negotiation meeting. You need to be fully on top of your 'case' and the arguments supporting it, and you should try to see it from the other person's point of view in order to anticipate the arguments that he or she is likely to put forward. In addition to this, be aware of any fears, attitudes or prejudices that may be affecting your judgement and that of your negotiating 'partner'.

In any negotiation there are two concerns: the case, or substance, which is being negotiated, and the relationship of the two parties. The combination of the two concerns is illustrated in Figure 4.1.

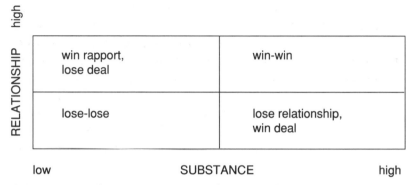

Figure 4.1   *The two concerns of negotiation*

This book is concerned with improving communications in order to improve relationships, and therefore takes the view that a solution that leads to a deterioration in relationships is unlikely to be a satisfactory one in the long term. The result to aim for is a win-win solution that satisfies both parties and ensures continuing good relationships. If this cannot be achieved then it is important to leave the door open for future discussions and opportunities to improve relationships.

Questions to bear in mind before the meeting are: will this be an exploratory or a decision-taking meeting (make sure both parties are agreed on this)? More specifically, what outcome are you seeking? A short-term or long-term solution? What are your minimum requirements? What does the other party want? What is the relative strength of the two parties? What is available for you to negotiate with? What is your fall-back position? It is important to have a good alternative to the one currently being negotiated; this is sometimes called a BATNA (Best Alternative to a Negotiated Agreement). It is also important to agree a time limit on the meeting, and on the whole negotiation.

If you have arranged the meeting, try to ensure that the environment is conducive to reaching an agreement. The room should be comfortable and well lit so that everyone can see the papers, and one another. Try to avoid sitting directly opposite your partner; although this means that you can make good eye contact, it tends to be a confrontational position. The best position is to sit at 90 degrees to each other, so that you can maintain reasonable eye contact but be able to look away from time to time as appropriate. If there are several of you then try to arrange things so that the two sides are not confronting each other across the table. You are more likely to reach agreement if you have established rapport, and this means helping people to feel relaxed and that although there may be disagreement over the problem, they themselves are respected and trusted.

During the negotiation, remember the assertiveness skills described in Chapter 2. Ask lots of questions, including hypothetical questions ('What would happen if I were to offer...?'), but avoid committing yourself to a position too early. Practise active listening. If you need time, say so. If you need further advice, say that you don't have the authority to make a concession and must refer it to a higher authority (the Finance Director, Board, etc). Use a few strong arguments rather than lots of weaker ones, and make sure that you have checked all the facts. Sound as if you are committed to a positive outcome, by saying 'Yes and...' rather than 'Yes but...' Be prepared to reconsider the whole package.

gender

There is evidence to suggest that men and women have different conversational styles, and that these can lead to misunderstanding, so if you have difficulty communicating with a member of the opposite sex, consider whether this may be the result of different styles. For example, men are generally better able to talk about their achievements, whereas women tend to play them down by saying things like 'Well, it wasn't anything very much' or 'I only...' Many men like to find practical solutions to problems; women give priority to showing empathy and establishing rapport. Many women try to find a roundabout way to give criticism, whereas men are more direct. These ideas are discussed in two books by Deborah Tannen, which are listed in Further Reading at the end of this book.

e-mail

This chapter considers good practice in using electronic mail (e-mail). It is based on the assumption that readers have a basic understanding of e-mail and how it works. If you do not, then I suggest that you look at other books (see Further Reading), find a class, ask a friend, or use the Help facilities in your software.

managing e-mail

E-mail needs to be managed carefully if it is not to get out of hand. Some messages are best kept as e-mail and can usually be organised into mailboxes or folders. You can sort them by date, sender, or subject by clicking on the bar at the top of each column, clicking again to create a different sort. Most mailers can filter incoming mail into designated mailboxes. Go through the mail regularly and weed out, sending unwanted items to the trash box. Scrolling up a screen if you haven't done it recently can be quite a surprise, and too many messages can cause a logjam. Replying to messages means that both the incoming message and the outgoing one are kept, and you may decide to delete one of these immediately.

You will help the receiver if you use the subject box to indicate not only the subject but also the purpose of your message, eg *request, information, report.*

E-mail is often the first thing we look at in the morning, but this can mean that the whole day is taken up with answering relatively routine enquiries while the important report remains to be written. Because of their immediacy, e-mail messages appear urgent even when they are not and in any case you need to be able to differentiate between things that are urgent and things that are important. Limit your e-mail use to, say, two or three times a day, and turn off the automatic e-mail alert facility, if you have one. You might consider delaying opening e-mail until mid-morning so that you won't get distracted from the important work you have to do.

Ongoing discussions can generate a lot of messages. Replying is very easy – all you need to do is click on 'reply' and the message will be turned around with the original sender's name in the recipient box. It helps your recipient to locate your reply if you put it at the top, not the bottom, of the incoming message. It's also good practice to delete unnecessary earlier messages from your reply, keeping only those that help to place your message in the appropriate context. You need to work out a system for keeping one complete set of messages, deleting unnecessary duplications.

This is not the place to go into detail about viruses, but beware – e-mail attachments are a common form of vehicle for transporting viruses, so make sure you have good virus detection software and as a general rule don't open anything that looks suspicious unless you can be sure that it is from a reputable sender.

what is special about e-mail?

E-mail is a powerful communication tool and has transformed office life. Message volume has increased dramatically over the past two or three years and looks set to continue. Its advantages are many, to the extent that some people find it addictive. One of the attributes that makes e-mail different from other forms of communication is that it is almost always faster than alternative forms of communication. This tends to add urgency to any communication, and the expectation of an immediate response. It may also lead to misunderstandings when the medium is immediate but the recipients are remote.

In character, e-mail is somewhere between an informal telephone call and a formal letter. The problem is that although people tend to use it informally messages can be retained as permanent records, unlike telephone conversations. Slang, careless writing, thoughtless comments, haphazard phrasing, all stand out in an e-mail. There is a tendency to put lots of dots and exclamation marks and question marks (..., !!!!!, ????) when one would be sufficient. It's all too easy to press the send key before you have given sufficient thought to your message, for example:

To: trainer <trainer@abc.com>
From: Other Mr A N <a.n.other@ucl.ac.uk>
Subject: RE: Finance Course

Bcc:
X-Attachments:

>the fee is quoted as as £265 ... it is unclear whether this includes one
>nights accomomodation... in which case it may not .... there is an online

>booking form at www.itsource.co.uk...... which may have more info..

>ALAN

>A N OTHER
>Administrator

Sarah, an administrator in a large company, has an example of this:

> When I first started using e-mail I treated it as the equivalent of a note scribbled at the bottom of a memo. It was quick and easy so I didn't bother to check for spelling mistakes or typos. Then I started to get similar-looking e-mails from colleagues and decided it looked really bad. So now I take much more care and quite often put outgoing messages in a queue so that I can check them one more time before sending them.

A shorthand is developing that is acceptable when used among colleagues who know one another well but is unacceptable in other contexts. Examples include omitting verbs, personal pronouns and other parts of speech: 'Report on desk. Will check.' Reducing complete words to two or three letters is also popular: 'Wd like inf asap.' Jargon should also be treated with care. Popular acronyms and abbreviations include NDA (non-disclosure agreement), B2C (business to customer), B2B (business to business), BCNU (be seeing you), LOL (laughing out loud), OIC (Oh I see), TTFN (Tata for now). There are concerns that 'e-mail English' is affecting other forms of written communication. The safest approach is to ensure that all your writing is clear and grammatical, and follows the general rules of good English described in Chapter 3.

One reason for the development of this shorthand is that many keyboard users do not possess keyboard skills. Training in keyboard skills is therefore increasingly important, and is to be recommended for everyone who spends substantial time at their computer. Proper use of the keyboard reduces the likelihood of developing repetitive strain injury.

E-mail encourages speedy and sometimes over-hasty working. There is a sense of urgency about an e-mail, and it is not uncommon for a sender to telephone a short while after sending one to see why it has not been responded to. Most systems have symbols to indicate urgency, which are helpful when used in moderation, but they can be abused. If you make all your messages urgent, people will gradually stop treating them as such, which will cause problems when something really is urgent.

E-mail can give you an excuse not to talk to someone. There are fears that the increasing use of electronic communication will affect our human relationships, so that we will become less sociable and find it more difficult to make friends and establish relationships, ultimately leading to social alienation and loneliness. Other people disagree, arguing that the Internet encourages friendship among people at a distance as it is quicker and cheaper to use e-mail rather than the telephone when communicating long-distance. You can use the Internet to find people with similar interests to yourself, and set up a regular correspondence with them. The fact that you don't need to worry about how you look and sound means that all parties can concentrate on the content of the message.

Written communications (letters, memos, reports, etc) can be said to be permanent, may be placed on record and have a responsible author. Face-to-face and telephone conversations, unless they are recorded, are non-permanent. Electronic messages may appear to be non-permanent but in fact they can be kept long-term, either electronically or printed out. Before being printed out, they can be amended to look more official than was ever intended. The content can be amended, and either printed, incorporated into a file, or forwarded to a third party, without the author knowing.

E-mail is highly interactive but, as we have seen, each interaction can result in a permanent record. Therefore, other forms of communication may be better at the early stages of a discussion when ideas are being put forward and opinions canvassed, leading to debate and discussion, activities that are normally most productive when carried out face to face.

Emma, who works in a busy marketing office, is aware of the problem of multiple e-mails on the same subject:

> Sometimes one enquiry leads to several messages going backwards and forwards between me and another person because I write for a piece of information and then remember something else I needed to know, and so I have to write again. So now I try to write a checklist first, or else telephone if I think there might be some discussion about what I'm wanting.

E-mail is not secure but can be retained, or printed out and subsequently produced in court. 'Unguarded language in messages can be the basis for constructive dismissal, defamation and discrimination claims. It can also create binding contracts where none were intended, breach third-party intellectual property rights, and disclose confidential information' (Temperton, 2000).

E-mail is cheap, particularly where mass communication is needed, and especially in organisations where the infrastructure is already in place. It allows you to communicate with hundreds of people all over the world. (It also means that they can communicate with you, resulting in spam, the electronic equivalent of junk mail.)

E-mail is democratic. This means that, potentially, everyone can write to everyone else, and mechanisms and procedures in offices that require individuals to communicate with senior staff only through their immediate line manager are becoming less viable. It is difficult for managers to check subordinates' e-mails for either content or style. It is also difficult for both managers and subordinates to keep track of one another, and different arrangements may need to be introduced, such as e-mail filters. Organisations are now developing some controls over e-mail, so that, for example, messages going outside the organisation may be checked. Under the 1998 Human Rights

Act, however, employees need to be informed if e-mail is monitored by employers.

E-mail can be time-consuming. It encourages procrastination – one message invariably leads to another, and a surprising amount of time can pass reading and responding to relatively trivial enquiries while the major report doesn't get written. The seemingly urgent takes precedence over the important. Mailboxes get bulkier as e-mail is used to request information that senders could find out for themselves, or to circulate information more widely than is necessary.

E-mail often generates an emotional response. This important issue deserves a section to itself.

e-mail and emotion

E-mail has the ability to generate emotional responses with surprising ease. E-mail used to convey anger or other negative emotions often results in misunderstanding or an escalation of strong messages resulting in damaged relationships; because of the speed with which messages can be sent this can happen surprisingly quickly.

The reasons for this are complex but include the following:

▓ Body language (tone of voice, facial expression) is lost.

▓ The immediacy, speed and informality of e-mail may lead to thoughtless responses (the time involved in re-reading and replying to a letter can take the edge off anger).

▓ Misunderstandings can be cleared up during the course of face-to-face conversation, and memories of these misunderstandings fade with time.

▓ Subtleties of humour and irony do not travel well by electronic means.

▓ There is an anonymity about e-mail so that people sometimes feel less constrained by the usual conventions of social discourse. Messages may be carelessly written and discourteous, or downright rude.

■ Having a row by e-mail is somehow safer, because it is at a distance.

The inability of e-mail to convey tone of voice or other forms of body language (see Chapter 1) means that your messages must be carefully worded to avoid any possibility of misunderstanding. Symbols are available on most systems to convey tone of voice – smiley faces, sad faces, flames, etc, but they are unsubtle and may distract the reader from your message. (A selection of symbols is given at the end of this chapter.) If you don't understand some of these conventions you may unwittingly upset people. Sarah again:

When I was still getting used to e-mail, a colleague sent me a draft report for comments. I had some criticisms about this draft, which I typed in just below the appropriate sections, and made the big mistake of putting my comments in capital letters, to differentiate from her writing. What I didn't realise was that capital letters signify shouting, so my poor colleague had my negative comments shouted at her, which she wasn't too pleased about. Also, I do think that if I had spoken to her or even written them in a formal letter I'd have been more thoughtful and diplomatic. E-mail encourages you to work too quickly sometimes.

Here is an example:

>To: manager@abc.com
>From: trainer@abc.com
>Re: Christmas
>
>At 11:11 14/12/2000 + 0000, you wrote:

>ANSWERS IN CAPITALS.
>Christmas is nearly here and I'd like to find a time next week for us to get together as a team for half an hour or so over coffee and a mince pie. Is this OK?

>
THAT'S NO GOOD FOR ME, I HAVE MEETINGS ON
MONDAY WHICH WILL TAKE UP MOST OF THE DAY
AND I HAVE ONLY JUST STARTED THINKING ABOUT
CHRISTMAS AND LEAVE AND SO FORTH. I AM
CONSIDERING TAKING TUESDAY 19TH AS LEAVE,
COMING IN ON WEDNESDAY 20TH AND THEN TAKING
ONE OR BOTH OF THURSDAY/FRIDAY 21/22 AS
LEAVE. SO WEDNESDAY WILL BE MY ONLY DAY FOR
OFFICE WORK. THERE ARE TOO MANY PARTIES
AROUND CHRISTMAS CAN'T WE MEET IN THE NEW
YEAR INSTEAD. MOST PEOPLE WOULD PREFER THIS.
>
>TRAINER
>>
>Manager

e-mail and stress

According to an article in *Personnel Today* (8 August 2000)
'simply dealing with the e-mail tide is a significant workplace
stress in its own right'. The article refers to a report by the
Institute of Management called *Taking the Strain* (February
2000), in which keeping up with e-mails is listed as the 10th
most stress-inducing activity of UK managers. It also
contributes to other factors, including 'constant interruptions',
'time pressures and deadlines' and 'poor internal communications'.

Although IT problems can cause difficulties, e-mail-related
stress is primarily a human problem, and some companies are
training their staff in its use. Others are developing guidelines
to cover the most common problems. Many large organisations
now have policies on e-mail usage, including statements such
as: 'All outgoing e-mail messages should be legal, decent,

honest and appropriate to their recipient.' Reference might then be made to what the organisation considers to be improper use, for example pornography, discrimination and harassment, and may be followed by more detailed examples of good practice, or 'netiquette', as it is now called.

There are signs that some people are becoming addicted, checking their e-mail compulsively throughout the day and always preferring e-mail to picking up the telephone, or having a face-to-face meeting. Examples are frequently quoted of colleagues at adjoining desks preferring to e-mail each other rather than speak. The result is a deterioration of personal relationships, leading to stress.

Here are suggested guidelines for good e-mail practice:

general

■ Encourage your organisation to develop an e-mail policy and good practice guidelines. If that is not possible, draw some up for use with your team.

■ Provide training, to include information on both the technology and the people issues.

■ Remember, if you don't control e-mail, it will control you.

sending

■ Do you need to say it? Would you go to the trouble of telephoning to say the same thing?

■ Assume any message you send is permanent. Never send a message unless you are prepared for it to be printed out, with your name attached.

■ Give thought to your audience. Is your message appropriate, and appropriately written? It is so easy to send copies to people that this is sometimes done without thinking – keep the number of recipients to a minimum.

■ You can't be sure which system your recipients will use to view your message, so you need to recognise that formatting may not survive. For this reason it is a good idea to treat all messages as plain text. (However, technological developments mean that this problem will decrease over the next year or two.)

■ Don't reply to a group if your message is intended for one individual.

■ Single-subject messages are to be preferred for ease of filing, retrieval and response.

■ Separate facts from opinion – this should reduce the number of misunderstandings.

■ Beware of humour, sarcasm, etc, and avoid them altogether unless you know the recipient very well. If you must express emotion, flag it as such (<Flame On>...<Flame Off>). However, be sure that your recipient understands the label. Also, be aware that labels in themselves can get in the way of the message.

■ Don't use all capitals, which are difficult to read and can indicate shouting.

■ Although shorthand is acceptable among friends, at work you are advised to write good grammatical English in your communications. Badly written, ungrammatical messages do not create a good impression, and will not be taken as seriously as more formal communications.

■ Try to be succinct. E-mail encourages chattiness, which is not always appropriate. Read through your messages and edit ruthlessly before pressing the 'send' button.

■ Be careful about sending attachments, preferring an html link if this is possible. If there are a large number of attachments it may be better to send them by post.

■ International e-mail correspondence creates further opportunities for misunderstandings and confusion, even in those countries with which we share the English language. Take particular care to write clearly, avoiding slang, jargon, humour and abbreviations. If you are writing with information about a meeting, use the 24-hour clock and write out days and months in full (eg 6 May 2001, not 6/5/01).

▦ Don't write while you are feeling emotional – or if you must, write the message but don't send it until you've calmed down and have had a chance to re-read it.

▦ Be careful about criticising people or organisations by e-mail. It's the problem of permanence again – a hasty remark on the telephone will not be recorded and may be forgotten, but this is not the case with e-mail.

▦ Consider queuing all but the most routine of your outgoing messages, so that you can read them over and decide if they are a) necessary, and b) appropriately worded. This is particularly sound advice late in the afternoon, especially Friday afternoon, when there is a danger of over-hasty responses in order to clear incoming messages.

responding to messages

▦ If you feel emotional after reading a message, give the sender the benefit of the doubt and assume that there has been a misunderstanding – poor choice of words, failure to 'label', etc. A good rule of thumb is – don't be too hasty. Have you read the message carefully? Are you quite sure you haven't misunderstood? Use the queuing system for your reply (ie write the message but don't send it immediately).

▦ If the matter seems complicated, consider responding by telephone, or in person. This will avoid the problem of a long string of e-mail messages.

▦ If you are going to be out of the office for more than a couple of days, check with your provider to see whether a message to this effect can be generated.

▦ Don't include the original message unnecessarily, but try to make your reply intelligible on its own.

forwarding e-mail
▓ Before forwarding a message, consider whether the original sender would wish you to do this.
▓ A lengthy distribution list at the head of a message lengthens the message unnecessarily, and you may wish to delete it. However, if you do this (or make other changes) it may be a good idea to indicate what you have done.
▓ If you forward only part of a message, you should indicate this.

junk mail
▓ Beware of giving your e-mail address too readily by subscribing to e-mail services or visiting Web sites.
▓ It is quite often easy to recognise junk mail before you open it, and therefore it can be deleted without wasting too much of your time.

some popular smileys (to be used with care!)

:-)	happy, smiling
:-(	sad, angry
:-o	surprise
;-)	winking
(:/)	sarcasm
:-<	very upset

references

Dear, I C B (comp) (1986) *Oxford English*, Oxford University Press

Gowers, E, rev Greenbaum, S and Whitcut, J (1986) *The Complete Plain Words*, 3rd edn, Oxford University Press

Mehrabian, A (1971) *Silent Messages*, pp 1–50, Wadsworth, Belmont, Calif

Temperton, E (2000) *People Management*, 22 June

further reading

Back, K and Back, K with Bates, T (1992) *Assertiveness at Work*, 2nd edn, McGraw-Hill, Maidenhead

Barker, A (2000) *Improve your Communication Skills*, Kogan Page, London

Concise Oxford English Dictionary (1999) 10th edn, Oxford University Press

Dear, I C B (comp) (1986) *Oxford English*, Oxford University Press

Flynn, N and Flynn, T (2000) *Writing Effective E-mail*, Kogan Page, London

Fowler, H W and Burchfield, R W (1996) *New Fowler's Modern English Usage*, Oxford University Press

Gowers, E, rev Greenbaum, S and Whitcut, J (1986) *The Complete Plain Words*, 3rd edn, Oxford University Press

Haynes, M (2000) *Make Every Minute Count*, 3rd edn, Kogan Page, London

Honey, P and Mumford, A (1983) *Using Your Learning Styles*, Peter Honey Publications, Maidenhead

Lawlor, M (1992) *Negotiating with Insight*, British Association for Commercial and Industrial Education (out of print)

Maitland, I (2000) *Make that Call!*, 2nd edn, Kogan Page, London

Parsloe, E and Wray, M (2000) *Coaching and Mentoring*, Kogan Page, London

Partridge, E, rev Whitcut, J (1999) *Usage and Abusage*, 3rd edn, Penguin, London

Plain English Campaign, PO Box 3, New Mills, High Peak, SK22 4QP (Web site: www.plainenglish.co.uk)

Shapiro, N and Anderson, R (1985) *Towards an Ethics and Etiquette for Electronic Mail*, R-3283-NSF/RC, RAND/ National Science Foundation, USA

Tannen, D (1992) *You Just Don't Understand*, Virago, London

Tannen, D (1994) *Talking from 9 to 5*, William Morrow & Co, New York

Whelan, J (2000) *E-mail at Work*, Pearson Education Limited, Harlow

Worrall, L and Cooper, C (1999) *The Quality of Working Life*, Institute of Management, London